FORTY YEARS ON

NEW ZEALAND–CHINA RELATIONS THEN, NOW, AND IN THE YEARS TO COME

A digest of the proceedings of the 40th-anniversary symposia held in Wellington and Beijing, September and December 2012

EDITED BY CHRIS ELDER

VICTORIA UNIVERSITY PRESS
for the New Zealand Contemporary China Research Centre

VICTORIA UNIVERSITY PRESS
Victoria University of Wellington
PO Box 600 Wellington
http://vup.victoria.ac.nz/

First published 2013

National Library of New Zealand Cataloguing-in-Publication Data

Forty years on : New Zealand-China relations, then, now and in
the years to come : a digest of the proceedings of the 40th anniversary
symposia held in Wellington and Beijing, September and December
2012 / edited by Chris Elder.
Includes bibliographical references and index.
ISBN 978-0-86473-915-5
1. New Zealand—Foreign relations—China—Congresses. 2. China—
Foreign relations—New Zealand—Congresses. I. Elder, Chris, 1947-
II. Title.
327.93051—dc 23

Printed by Printstop, Wellington

CONTENTS

PREFACE

New Zealand and China established diplomatic relations on 22 December 1972. To mark the 40th anniversary of the establishment of relations, two symposia were held, one in each capital. The Wellington symposium took place on 5 September 2012, and the Beijing event followed on 4 December 2012.

The symposia were organised jointly by three institutions: the New Zealand Contemporary China Research Centre, the New Zealand Institute of International Affairs, and the Chinese Academy of Social Sciences. Contributors and participants included political leaders, government officials, academics, business people, journalists, and others associated with the development of the relationship. Discussion ranged over the growth of political links, the trade and economic relationship, cultural and people-to-people exchanges, the effects of migration, and the two countries' interests in the wider Asia-Pacific region. It reviewed the developments of the past 40 years, and it also looked towards the prospects for the years ahead.

This publication offers a digest of the two days' deliberations, expressed in the words of the participants. Key points from the often discursive discussions have been marshalled so far as possible into broad subject areas. While in some cases the texts of formal presentations are provided in full or in part, in many others the observations derive from commentaries on or reactions to those papers. Speakers are identified, but it has not been thought necessary to record into which session on which day the remarks fall. Full programmes for the Wellington and Beijing symposia, and details of those participating, are included at annex.

INTRODUCTION

It is interesting to speculate what a colloquium on New Zealand–China relations would have looked like 40 years ago. Certainly not anything like the two upon which this report is based. There would have been little to discuss, few people qualified to discuss it, and not too many willing to give up a whole day to follow the deliberations.

Fast-forward to 2012, and the situation could hardly be more different. The two seminars organised by Victoria University of Wellington's New Zealand Contemporary China Research Centre and the New Zealand Institute of International Affairs in collaboration with the Chinese Academy of Social Sciences were able to call upon a wide range of expertise from both countries. Contributors' views were backed up by considerable research and solid analysis. In Wellington, such was the interest that it was necessary to change to a larger venue, and in the end to turn people away. Far from there being not much to talk about, both the 10 September seminar in Wellington and its 4 December counterpart in Beijing showed no sign of having exhausted the exploration of their topic even after a full day's focused discussion.

The difference between what might have been the situation 40 years ago, and the reality of today, is a measure of the level of growth and change in both countries, and in the relationship between them. The symposia examined the course of that growth, from small beginnings in the immediate aftermath of the 1972 establishment of diplomatic relations, through to the burgeoning relationship of today, where China has become New Zealand's second largest trading partner, a key source of immigrants and tourists, and an indispensable interlocutor on regional and international security. While differences of scale mean that China looms far larger for New Zealand than will ever be the case in reverse, New Zealand has achieved a level of recognition in China as a reliable supplier, a useful sounding board, and a frank and independent participant in the affairs of the Asia-Pacific region.

It would be too much (or too little) to hope that the views expressed and the conclusions drawn in the two 40th anniversary symposia would all coincide, or even point roughly in the same direction. They do not. New Zealand should open its doors to Chinese investment; New Zealand should be circumspect. China/United States relations will get better; they will get worse. The China market is one that requires long cultivation; it is one where deals can be done overnight. If everyone were in agreement, it would hardly be worth publishing an account of proceedings. As it is, there exists material for a robust debate. The intention of this publication is to set some parameters for that debate, in order to stimulate further discussion of the past, present, and future of a relationship that has emerged as one of central importance to New Zealand.

Rt. Hon. John Key, Prime Minister of New Zealand, delivers the opening address.

KEYNOTE ADDRESS

OPENING ADDRESS TO THE CHINA SYMPOSIUM, 5 SEPTEMBER 2012

At the outset of the first colloquium, the New Zealand Prime Minister, Rt. Hon. John Key, delivered a speech tracing the evolution of New Zealand's relationship with China. That established the context for the discussions that went on through the rest of the day, and continued in Beijing.

Rt. Hon. John Key, Prime Minister of New Zealand

Ministers and Members of Parliament, Ambassador Xu, members of the Diplomatic Corps, ladies and gentlemen. Thank you for inviting me here today.

Can I start by acknowledging the Contemporary China Research Centre at Victoria University and the New Zealand Institute of International Affairs who are hosting this event.

This seminar today marks the 40th anniversary of diplomatic relations between New Zealand and China. I welcome the opportunity to reflect on those 40 years. I also welcome the opportunity to look forward, and to consider the possibilities that lie ahead for our two countries.

Relations between New Zealand and China are very good. We have extremely good trade links, which each year go from strength to strength. Our people are regular visitors to each other's countries. New Zealand is home to many people who have come here from China. In recent years, New Zealand has had three Chinese Members of Parliament – two of them from my own party, the National Party. And our governments meet often and work together effectively.

In 2012, Vice Premier Li described the relations between our two governments as "at its best ever". It has certainly come a very long way since 1949. That was in the early throes of the Cold War. And New Zealand and China soon found themselves on opposite sides in the conflict in Korea.

But in 1972, Richard Nixon made his ground-breaking visit to China. That, on top of the outstanding diplomacy conducted by Henry Kissinger and Zhou Enlai, provided the opportunity for 28 countries, including New Zealand and Australia, to officially recognise the Beijing government. New Zealand recognised China in December 1972, establishing the basis for New Zealand's enduring "one China" policy.

Yet even during those early years, from 1949 to 1972, when the country was largely closed to foreigners, a handful of New Zealanders left their mark on China. The most famous was, of course, Rewi Alley. Alley was a Cantabrian who went to China in 1927 and spent the rest of his life there – a total of 60 years. While working in Shanghai factories and travelling into the interior of the country, he became aware of the plight of ordinary Chinese peasants and workers. During the war against Japan he helped establish thousands of small cooperative factories. He founded schools. And he was a prolific author and international publicist for the Communist government, while continuing to hold a New Zealand passport.

The photographer Brian Brake also visited China, in the late 1950s. His photographs, taken during the period of the Great Leap Forward, form a unique record of a turbulent period. The New Zealand Government is supporting Te Papa to tour a collection of Brake photographs from this era, in partnership with the National Museum of China. They will be on display in Beijing at the time of the 40th anniversary.

Since the establishment of diplomatic relations, New Zealand and China have developed a broad and substantial relationship that is among New Zealand's most important. We have different cultures, different histories and different political traditions. So we often have a different perspective on things. However, we are able to express our views with openness, honesty and respect. That is an important indicator of our positive intent over 40 years.

This level of personal engagement by New Zealanders in China was possible in part because the New Zealand government relaxed travel bans against China before many other Western countries. It also relaxed trade bans. In 1956, New Zealand lifted trade embargoes imposed on China during the Korean War. Wool, tallow, hides and skins were New Zealand's main exports in those days, but trade flows remained relatively small. Exporters found it difficult linking buyers and sellers across very different economic systems, and connections were limited. In 1972, bilateral trade between New Zealand and China totalled only $1.7 million, and there were no air links between our two countries.

To a New Zealander in 1972, China would have seemed an unknown, mysterious country of close to a billion people. And it's hard to believe New Zealand figured highly in the minds of most Chinese. So much has changed, then, in 40 years. Since the establishment of diplomatic relations, New Zealand and China have developed a broad and substantial relationship that is among New Zealand's most important. We have different cultures, different histories and different political traditions. So we often have a different perspective on things. However, we are able to express our views with openness, honesty and respect. That is an important indicator of our positive intent over 40 years.

Our trade relationship, in particular, has been a huge success, and momentum has grown very quickly in recent years. In part, that is because of China's ever-increasing importance in the global economy. In 1981, when several pioneering New Zealand businesses formed the New Zealand China Trade Association, China accounted for 2.3 per cent of global GDP. By 2011 this had risen to 14.4 per cent. Rapidly rising living standards, increasing urbanisation and a shift to higher-protein diets have supported demand for New Zealand products.

But our booming commerce is also due to the fact that New Zealand and China have worked hard to develop our trade relationship over a number of years. New Zealand was the first country to recognise that China had established a market economy, in 2004. We were the first country to agree bilaterally to China becoming a member of the World Trade Organisation. And in 2008, our two countries signed an historic free trade agreement.

Since then, trade between us has grown exponentially. New Zealand's goods exports to China have trebled in only four years, and China is now our second-largest export market. Dairy and wood products are the largest export commodities, followed by meat and wool. New Zealand now exports more than ten times the value of product to China every day than we did in the whole of 1972. Chinese demand has done much to support the New Zealand economy over the last few years.

China is also Australia's largest export destination, chiefly in mineral resources, providing further indirect benefits for New Zealand, given that Australia is our top trading partner. China is also New Zealand's biggest source of imported goods. Two-way trade in 2011 totalled $13.3 billion and is rising all the time. Our countries are certainly on track to achieve the goal Premier Wen and I set in 2010, of doubling our trade to $20 billion per annum by 2015.

Our investment relationship with China is much smaller than our trade relationship, but that, too, is growing. China is New Zealand's 11th largest investor with $1.8 billion of investment in 2011. In particular, Chinese firms have made investments in New Zealand forestry, manufacturing and agriculture. China is also investing in New Zealand government bonds, contributing to the record low borrowing rates New Zealand currently enjoys. New Zealand is seen as a relatively safe haven in these difficult times and Chinese authorities have wanted to diversify their international bond holdings.

Recently, there have been some encouraging examples of New Zealand firms investing in China. Fonterra, for example, has significant plans to increase the number of farms it operates in China, with a roughly NZ$50 million investment per farm. And high-tech firm Rakon opened a US$35 million factory in Chengdu last year.

People-to-people links between New Zealand and China are also strong. Chinese tourism to New Zealand only commenced in earnest at the end of the 1990s but is increasingly significant. Last year Chinese tourist numbers grew by 33 per cent. That number will continue to grow under a new air services agreement that was agreed earlier this year.

A lot of young Chinese people also come to New Zealand to study. Since the 1990s, China has been New Zealand's largest education market. New Zealand is today providing a quality educational experience and pastoral care to around 23,000 Chinese students, and we are aiming to grow that further.

And many Chinese want to stay permanently in New Zealand, rather than just visiting. China is the second largest source of migrants to New Zealand, behind the United Kingdom. The next census is likely to show a resident population of Chinese in New Zealand of close to 200,000 people. But in relative terms, a greater proportion of New Zealanders actually live in China, rather than vice versa. More than 3,000 New Zealanders are living in China, which is not insignificant compared to our total population of only 4.4 million.

But the relationship between New Zealand and China is not just about people-to-people and trade relations. From time to time, New Zealand hosts military ship visits from China. We work together in regional organisations such as APEC, and on disaster relief. China was one of several countries to send urban search and rescue teams to assist New Zealand in the immediate aftermath of the Christchurch earthquake, and to donate money for reconstruction. We are very grateful for that assistance. New Zealand has also aided China after natural disasters, including the great Sichuan earthquake in 2008.

And just last week at the Pacific Islands Forum, we announced a new partnership between the Cook Islands, China and New Zealand that will deliver an improved water mains system in Rarotonga. This new piece of infrastructure will ensure communities and businesses have access to clean drinking water. It will mean a better quality of life for the people of the Cook Islands and it will help promote economic growth. The project is the first time New Zealand has worked with China to deliver a major development initiative in the Pacific. It is an example of how we can work together to get the most benefit from our aid programmes in the Pacific.

Looking forward, it is safe to assume that current trends will continue. The centre of gravity of global economic activity will keep shifting from the Atlantic to the Asia-Pacific region. Europe will remain a vital outlet for some of our highest value exports, but our biggest growing markets will be around the Pacific basin. In that environment, New Zealand has a lot to offer. We are a reliable, competitive and high-quality source of food. We have technical knowledge and expertise that can help countries in this region develop, build infrastructure and add value to their natural resources. We can deliver a world-class education to the next generation of leaders across Asia and the Pacific. And we are a great place to visit, see wonderful scenery and play a few rounds of golf.

We have lots of things we can sell to other countries, but we also want to see New Zealand businesses forming productive partnerships with Asian and Pacific businesses across the region. There are many new fields of opportunity for New Zealand businesses and people to explore. To operate successfully in this region over coming decades they will need to have a good understanding of China, and of Asia in general.

In February I launched the NZ Inc China Strategy. The strategy is about getting greater efficiency and effectiveness across all government agencies that work in, and with, China. And it's about developing more targeted and cohesive services to help successful businesses develop and grow in China. We want to be transparent about our bilateral interests, and get on with advancing them.

The China Strategy has a strong trade and economic focus. And it has been developed with industry groups, businesses and organisations involved in building New Zealand's relationship with China. The Strategy sets out ambitious, high-level goals, together with actions to achieve them. The five goals are:

- to retain and build a strong, resilient political relationship
- to double two-way trade to $20 billion by 2015, as I mentioned before
- to grow services trade including education services by 20 per cent, and grow the value of tourism exports by 60 per cent, all by 2015
- to increase investment to reflect our growing commercial relationship
- and to grow high-quality science and technology collaborations with China that generate commercial collaborations.

I'm pleased to say the Strategy has been positively received in New Zealand and in China. It's an important document. Our relationship with China is critical to achieving the Government's aim of building a competitive and more productive economy.

One of the immediate outcomes of the Strategy was the formation of the New Zealand China Council. The Council brings together New Zealanders who are engaged in China from across a whole range of fields, including people in the business, academic, science, cultural and education communities. As the Council's chair, Sir Don McKinnon, put it, the Council will operate as an umbrella organisation stretching across the breadth of New Zealand's relationship with China, and not leaving anyone in the shade. I think this is a significant further step in building on what is already a very strong relationship in many areas.

The China Strategy also reinforces the Government's commitment to ministerial engagement, both as hosts and visitors to China, to build important relationships with China's leadership.

As Prime Minister, I made my first official visit to China in 2009, where I met

President Hu Jintao and Premier Wen Jiabao. And I am hoping to visit China again later this year, to meet the new Chinese leadership. I also hope to launch the New Zealand China Council's inaugural Partnership Forum in Beijing. I think that would be a fitting way to mark the 40th anniversary of a significant relationship, which has a proud history and can look forward to an even better future.

I am confident that, with all of your support, we will continue to see New Zealand's relationship with China go from strength to strength over the coming years.

Thank you.

—Rt. Hon. John Key

PART I
RECOGNITION AND THE GROWTH OF THE POLITICAL RELATIONSHIP

The beginnings

饮水思源

When you drink the water, remember the source

The Walding mission

New Zealand and China established diplomatic relations through an exchange of letters in New York on 22 December 1972. Three months later, on 28 March 1973, the Associate Minister of Foreign Affairs, Hon. Joe Walding, led a mission to Beijing to establish direct contact at ministerial level.

We didn't fly into China – 40 years ago there were no international flights into China, except maybe once or twice a week from places like Hanoi. There was effectively one point of entry, from Hong Kong by train to Lowu. The capitalist train ended there, and you had to carry your bags across the bridge that marked the border. It was really a step into the unknown – most of us carried food supplies, because there was no certainty that China would be able to feed us. At Lowu, elderly ladies did good business selling rolls of toilet paper at vastly inflated prices on the understanding that this was an article unobtainable in New China. As it turned out, both commodities were in ample supply, especially the food, then, as now, a big weapon in winning over foreign delegations.

The food in fact began as soon as we crossed the border. We were greeted by a Vice-Chairman of the Canton Revolutionary Committee, and invited to a substantial lunch while we waited to board the train to Canton. Through the dining room windows, we had our first glimpse of Communist China, in the form of a sleepy little village beside a duck pond. The name of the village was Shenzhen, its population at that time was about 25,000. Since then, of course, it's grown a bit – it's now rather more than 14 million, and Shenzhen has attracted $30 billion of foreign investment.

Then it was all aboard the People's express and on to Canton, then by plane to Peking. The incident I remember most from that train journey was Bryce Harland producing a fur hat with ear flaps to show how he was going to cope with the North China climate, and Mr Walding saying, with an eye to the Deputy Chairman of the

Canton Revolutionary Committee, "You'd better be careful with that hat, Bryce, or they'll think you're a Russian and shoot you."

Surprisingly, that rambling account contains within it the seeds of all the main considerations that conditioned diplomatic relations between New Zealand and China at the time they were first set in place.

The **first** is China's considerable isolation at the time. It really was a closed society. It had little communication with the outside world, either physical in the form of air and rail links, or in terms of diplomatic communication. Remember this was a country that had been out of touch with many countries for about 20 years and was just emerging from the Cultural Revolution.

The **second** is the remarkable level of ignorance about conditions inside the country – even so basic a thing as food supplies. This was a consequence of the lack of communication and of course it went both ways. After the delegation arrived in Peking and had their talks with Mr Walding's opposite number, Vice Foreign Minister Qiao Guanhua, there was a report on page 3 of the People's Daily the following day. What was more remarkable was that on page 1 of the same newspaper was the report of another meeting with another New Zealand delegation – Premier Zhou Enlai held a friendly conversation with Comrade VG Wilcox, General Secretary of The New Zealand Communist Party. Excuse me? Vic Wilcox? This was a party that had managed to garner a grand total of 364 votes nation-wide in the 1969 general election. But for more than 10 years it had it had been feted in Beijing as a serious alternative to Labour and National.

The **third** is that China was not yet on a path of rapid economic development. The impulse that created wealthy new cities like Shenzhen was still in the future. In terms of its commitment to foreign trade, there was still a vigorous debate going on about whether China should become part of the world trading system, and subject to its influence, or whether it should maintain the closed economy which had to a considerable extent been imposed upon it over the previous 20 years.

The **fourth** is, as Mr Walding shrewdly pointed out, that Chinese foreign policy was totally dominated by fear of the threat posed by the Soviet Union. There was real concern about the possibility of a pre-emptive nuclear strike by Moscow. All the buildings we inspected [as possible Embassy premises] came with fully-functioning fall-out shelters. Documents that have become public since the fall of the Soviet Union suggest that it was by no means an irrational fear.

The Soviet Threat was to the fore in the presentation of Vice-Minister Qiao Guanhua, when he and Mr Walding met at the Great Hall of The People. Two main concerns were raised on the New Zealand side. One was the possibility of China providing material support for insurgencies in Southeast Asia – at least we called them "insurgencies" – the Chinese called them "revolutionary movements", but emphasised the fundamental position that revolution could not be exported. The other was New Zealand's opposition to nuclear testing, whether in the atmosphere or below ground.

New Zealand's recognition of the People's Republic of China was:

Long delayed

Ormond Wilson, the former Labour MP, led a delegation on a fact-finding tour to China in 1956. They were invited to a reception with then Premier Zhou Enlai, and in the course of their conversation stumblingly expressed the hope that New Zealand would soon move to establish relations with the People's Republic of China. "Well," Zhou Enlai said comfortingly, "I think that China can wait."

Controversial

I recall in 1972 I was a junior electoral chairman for the National Party when we were swept from power. Labour came in with a policy commitment to open the path to diplomatic relations with China, and moved quickly on that. In opposition we wondered what would happen. With the benefit of reflection what Kirk was doing was recognising the reality that a quarter of mankind existed.

—*Sir Douglas Kidd*

Inevitable

The event that finally provided the catalyst for recognition was the election of the Kirk Government in New Zealand, but by then there was a certain inevitability about it. China was admitted to the United Nations in 1971, despite New Zealand's furious opposition. Canada had recognised, the Kissinger and Nixon visits had taken place, Whitlam had travelled to Beijing as leader of the Australian Opposition, and was clearly going to follow Canada's example when he was elected Prime Minister. All that Labour's victory in New Zealand did was save the National Government from having to perform an embarrassing volte-face.

In 1986 George Laking, who was Secretary of Foreign Affairs at the time of recognition, wrote to my friend and colleague Michael Green, saying that "The process was inevitable and by the end of 1972, even before Norman Kirk had actually taken office, there was no practicable alternative to recognition. Indeed, even if there had not been a change of Government, the same situation would have applied. For many months before the election I had been involved in a series of negotiations leading up to that kind of climate. Holyoake had accepted the inevitability of it but like Peter Fraser in 1949 he did not want the question of recognition to be an issue in the election, and perhaps more importantly, he wanted to be able to lead the first Governmental Commission to China in 1973".

—*Chris Elder*

It's important to note that Mr Walding conducted these discussions as Associate Minister of Foreign Affairs, not as Minister of Overseas Trade, although he did also meet with China's trade minister Bai Xiangguo. From the beginning it was recognised that good trade relations would only come on the back of a good political relationship. There is confusion sometimes that Mr Walding led a trade mission to China in 1973. The confusion arises from the fact that Mr Walding did lead a trade mission to China in 1973. He in fact travelled to China twice in the same year, first with the Ministerial Mission in March and then again with a trade mission in October.

The other important principle to come out of the first discussions was China's insistence that political and diplomatic contacts were not enough. Qiao moved quickly to suggest other ways in which the relationship could be strengthened – sporting and cultural exchanges, student exchanges and so on. To kick things off he proposed sending a Chinese acrobatic troupe to New Zealand.

That was a salutary reminder to New Zealand that China saw the relationship in the round. We had in fact already made an effort to get relations on the cheap – if you look at the communiqué establishing relations it includes quite specific language on setting up of embassies and exchanging ambassadors as early as practical. That was a Chinese response to the New Zealand suggestion that it would be enough to establish relations, and minor details like exchanging embassies could come later.

—*Chris Elder*

An early scorecard

What was achieved in those early years? How different did the shape of the relationship look at the end of the term of the first ambassador, three years after the formal establishment of relations? For an answer I am indebted to Bryce Harland's farewell dispatch.

In terms of political relations, Bryce points out that New Zealand had been able to enter into a dialogue with China on the issues of importance to us. Those issues at that time included Chinese nuclear testing, support for communist insurgents in Southeast Asia, and China's relations with the island countries of the South Pacific. In all of these, the nature of the Soviet threat was a constant. It's a dialogue that has continued to this day, though of course the issues have changed.

Speaking of trade, Bryce comments that this has been one of the main benefits of establishing diplomatic relations. The total volume of trade increased sixfold in three years, to the unprecedented level of $38 million. It seems pretty small beer compared to the levels of trade that are now being reached, but it was seen as the affirmation of a principle that I believe still to be true, that a favourable political climate is a necessary condition for the development of a fruitful long-term trading relationship.

The third area of activity that Bryce singles out for particular comment at the three-year mark is that of bilateral exchanges. He points to the importance of high-level visits. He points also to the importance of exchanges at other levels – we had by 1975 already set in place exchanges of doctors, scientists, students, journalists, sports teams and the entire National Youth Orchestra.

He points finally to what has been achieved through people-to-people exchanges – visits by private citizens. This was a time when we knew very little of China, and the years of lack of contact had left a residue of suspicion. Bryce comments that "Not many New Zealanders who come here go away thinking that China is either Heaven on Earth or Hell. By seeing the country and meeting the people themselves, they at least begin to shake off the prejudices that have bedevilled relations between the two countries in the past, and to prepare themselves for facing the realities of the future."

—*Chris Elder*

Hon. Joe Walding meets Premier Zhou Enlai at the Great Hall of the People, 31 March 1973.

The first Prime Ministerial visit to China: Rt. Hon. Robert Muldoon and Mrs Muldoon on the Great Wall, May 1976. (Photo: National Archives).

The growing relationship

日新月异

New every day, and different every month

40 years of relations between China and New Zealand

The year 2012 is important for both China and New Zealand, since this year is the 40th anniversary of diplomatic relations between the People's Republic of China and New Zealand. During the 40 years of official bilateral relations, we have both made various achievements and pushed bilateral relations to a higher and more mature level.

Politically, we have established an annual leaders' dialogue, supported by regular high-level exchanges.

Economically, the structural complementarities and the Sino New Zealand Free Trade Agreement (FTA) have placed bilateral trade within a healthy framework with rapid development. As a result, China is becoming one of the most important trade partners for New Zealand, the second largest one following Australia in general bilateral trade, New Zealand's second largest export market and largest source of imports. Meanwhile, Chinese investment is increasing fast.

Socially, China has become New Zealand's third largest tourist market and one of the most significant sources of foreign students.

Culturally, as exchanges increase, New Zealand's culture and natural beauty fascinate the Chinese public more and more, with the additional impact of movies – the Lord of the Rings, Avatar.

Therefore, Sino–New Zealand relations have been defined as the best in history, a win-win cooperation model between the West and China, a good example for coexistence between different political systems, stages of development and cultural backgrounds.

Relations between China and New Zealand have a history of at least 200 years, starting with people-to-people contact through business, migration, culture etc. China and New Zealand are geographically separated so that historically, bilateral understanding was limited or indirect. However, we have built positive perceptions of one another, perhaps for the following reasons (at least on the Chinese side).

A. Although our experiences in building a modern state were very different, we both achieved national independence at almost the same time. As a western nation, New Zealand is far removed from the centre of the West in terms of location, lacking a negative historical record, and gradually building more links with East Asia.

B. Although New Zealand is within the club of developed nations, it has a strong agricultural industry, which is attractive to Chinese since China has historically been famous for its agricultural civilisation. New Zealand's animal husbandry and dairy products have been very popular in China.

C. Although it has been difficult to have direct and regular people-to-people exchanges in the past, individual cases have been influential in shaping public views of one another. The story of Rewi Alley in China, for example, has had a very positive impact upon Chinese attitudes towards New Zealand, since he was in China for several decades from the Chinese civil war through to New China, at a time when China was undergoing a remarkable transition.

D. Although we have different ideologies, China's efforts to return to the international community through reform and opening up to the world started in the late 1970s, and regional development, led by Japan, has been dynamic over the same period, eventually leading to the East Asian economy becoming a bright point in the world.

Panellists at the opening session of the Beijing Symposium, held in the meeting hall of the Chinese Academy of Social Sciences.

Strategy and Structure

Our bilateral relations over 40 years have made us more relevant to the regional framework, bringing similar perceptions and needs.

The establishment of diplomatic relations between China and New Zealand in the early 1970s saw China getting political recognition from the West for its different system of government. However, China had to carry out a policy of reform because of the internal political and economic difficulties caused by the 10-year-long Cultural Revolution, and it had to open its doors to the world as well.

Sino–New Zealand relations have been defined as the best in history, a win-win cooperation model between the West and China, a good example for coexistence between different political systems, stages of development, and cultural backgrounds.

China's priority was to rescue and develop its economy, so the main purpose of its foreign policy was first to maintain regional stability and security in neighbouring areas, and secondly to seek economic relations with the global market on the basis of its regional experiences. Thus, the the two sides had the opportunity to move in the same direction at the same time within the region. Both China and New Zealand gave political support to Southeast Asia over the issue of Cambodia, and economically New Zealand was readjusting its economic structures and relationships in the 1970s and 1980s because of the world economic crisis, and because its most important traditional political and economic partner, the United Kingdom, joined the European Union. East Asia was becoming a common focus for us.

In the 1990s, when the Chinese economy and social development were stable and provided a basis of confidence for becoming more deeply involved in regional cooperation, China took part in the ASEAN Dialogue, Asia-Pacific Economic Cooperation (APEC), the ASEAN Regional Forum (ARF), and ASEAN and China, Japan and Korea (ASEAN +3). New Zealand is also a member of most of these groups. And in a new century, China joined in the ASEAN and China Free Trade Agreement in 2010, the Treaty of Amity and Cooperation, the Southeast Asia Nuclear Free Arrangement, and the East Asia Summit, which includes New Zealand. Taken together with the bilateral FTA in 2008, Sino–New Zealand relations have been upgraded with the buildup of regional structures.

—*Prof. Han Feng*

Substantial progress

Forty years ago, New Zealand joined a great number of countries, developed Western countries in particular, in establishing diplomatic relations with China after its lawful seat in the United Nations was restored. Substantial progress has since been made across the board. Many of us here are personal witnesses to this process.

I became China's ambassador to NZ in 2005 and presented my credentials in early 2006. Later that year, the leaders of the two countries reached an important agreement to build a comprehensive cooperation for mutual benefit in the 21st century, bringing China–NZ relations to a new stage. Basing their relations solidly on equality, political trust and full respect for each other's vital interests, the two countries have enjoyed regular exchanges of high-level visits and conducted close consultation and coordination on major international and regional issues.

On the economic front, two-way trade has increased nearly a thousandfold and bilateral cooperation in a whole range of areas has made impressive headway thanks in part to China's reform, opening up and modernisation drive. What is worth special mention is that in a display of vision and courage, the two countries worked collaboratively to accomplish something that has never been done before: the conclusion of a free trade agreement between a developed country and the world's largest developing country. So far, New Zealand remains the only Western country that has signed an FTA with both China and its Hong Kong SAR. The agreement has led to an extraordinary expansion of trade between the two countries despite difficulties and challenges brought by the international financial crisis.

A robust growth has been registered in China–NZ cultural and people-to-people relations. In addition to their 29 pairs of sister-city relationships, China has become New Zealand's largest source of overseas students and second largest source of inbound tourists. When I was the ambassador, I helped open the first Confucius Institute in Auckland. Now, there are three Confucius Institutes and eight Confucius Classes across New Zealand, and more and more primary and secondary schools in the country have put the Chinese language into their programmes. The greater traffic of exchanges at the level of ordinary individuals is not only an indicator of healthy state-to-state relations but also an indispensable element for their steady and long-term growth.

—Ambassador Zhang Yuanyuan

Managing the relationship

纲举目张

Hold the net's headrope, the rest will follow

The four firsts

One of the descriptions of New Zealand commonly used by Chinese officials in my time – from Hu Jintao and Wen Jiabao onwards – is that the New Zealand is the country of the Four Firsts. It is a tag coined by China, but enthusiastically repeated by New Zealanders

Why was New Zealand the "first"? Was it deliberate? Was it good diplomacy? Was it simply fortuitous? What lay behind the decisions that lead to these "four firsts"? I want to look at the key decision points that led to these "Firsts" being agreed, in particular the first two, and consider what lessons there might be for the ongoing management of our relationship.

The first "First": New Zealand being the first Western economy to agree bilateral terms for China's accession to the WTO, goes back to August 1997. China had lodged its application in 1986. Each of the 142 members, or however many are there were then, had to agree terms for China's accession. Our trade negotiators are quick to point out that the first Western country to enter into negotiations with China was in fact New Zealand in 1997, when no Western country had signed off.

Long Yongtu's negotiating team was under considerable pressure to show progress. It was on the eve of the 15th Party Congress, and there needed to be evidence that the WTO bid, on which so much rested, was moving in the right direction. New Zealand was pretty far down the road in our negotiations, with, as usual, dairy being the main sticking point. In July 1997 Long had to get someone to sign up, in the face of a concerted Western position that all holding off would increase pressure on China to make concessions. Long had a meeting with the New Zealand delegation in Geneva and deliberately made an offer that was aimed at getting New Zealand to be the first to conclude those access talks.

The important thing here is what New Zealand did. We recognised that this was a good deal; that the argument for not closing the deal would be based on relations with third parties as the deal on the table was clearly in New Zealand's interest to sign. The advice from our Geneva mission was categorical: that the deal was in our interest, and that we should move quickly to ensure that we were the first to agree terms. Within two weeks of Long's meeting with Ambassador Wade Armstrong in Geneva, the New Zealand trade minister was in Beijing signing off on the agreement.

There's a footnote to this. For we didn't in fact agree. We agreed market access terms, but tariff quota arrangements were being negotiated not with MOFTEC but with the old State Development and Planning Commission, not on an individual country but on an across-the-board basis. So our agreement signed in Beijing was "subject to satisfactory terms being agreed on tariff quota administration for wool". That argument continued until the end of 2000, by which time New Zealand was among the last countries holding out on a final tick off!

Let's turn to the second "First". I would argue that the second, third, and fourth are all part of the FTA negotiation. For New Zealand the second "First" dates back to mid-2003, when New Zealand started to take seriously the idea of an FTA negotiation with China.

- China had joined the WTO nearly two years earlier, and the process of economic reform that this had been central to was reinforced at the Party Congress in late 2002, and the NPC a few months earlier. A new Commerce Minister, Bo Xilai, was in office.
- One aspect of China's WTO accession deal was very strongly objected to: the United States-led insistence that in respect of dumping and trade remedies China would be treated differently from all other WTO members. Getting rid of this was primarily a political issue for China.
- On the New Zealand side we had begun a push for FTA agreements to give a push to regional economic liberalisation, both for its own sake and to underpin Doha Round progress – starting from the New Zealand/Singapore deal in 2000. That effort to expand the range of regional negotiating partners had had us looking closely at options with Taiwan.
- Australia had signed its FTA with the United States, and was examining whether there were possibilities with China.

New Zealand had been considering the possibility of pursuing a free trade agreement with Taiwan, when we received a signal from China, through Ambassador Chen Mingming in Wellington, that we should instead think about working towards an FTA with China. The New Zealand Government was rapidly persuaded that seeking a full FTA should be part of the goals behind work towards a TECF. China made it very clear, however, that any movement towards an FTA negotiation could only occur on the basis of China's being recognised as a market economy.

In September 2003, then President Hu Jintao visited Wellington, and set out the Chinese position clearly in a meeting with Prime Minister Helen Clark. On the basis of these preliminary discussions, at the second round of the TECF talks in Beijing in April 2004, New Zealand offered a deal whereby recognition of China as a market economy would clear the way for substantive negotiation towards a free trade agreement.

So what are the key points from this?

- New Zealand may be the country of the "Four Firsts", but in no case were these a unilateral decision on New Zealand's part: they resulted from both sides having clear interests at stake, albeit asymmetrical, that would allow a benefit for both.
- while the "Four Firsts" might largely be seen in New Zealand as economic issues, the economic benefits flow from acutely political decisions.
- for New Zealand the benefits from the "Four Firsts" came from us breaking ranks with "Western" positions: they highlight the importance in our relationship with China of identifying our national interest ahead of any "like-minded" solidarity.
- China's asks of us required not just an affirmative response, but a speedy response – in the main because of its domestic political pressures. We had sufficient flexibility within our system to be able to provide that.
- New Zealand had to be first to get on the agenda at all. In a relationship between two countries of such different size and influence the smaller party will always have limited opportunity to influence the shape of the relationship. It is always up to the smaller country to identify opportunity and act while the window is open.
- Don't discount the importance a small country like New Zealand can have in advancing what China sees to be its interests – and in doing so advancing our own.

—Tony Browne

The Four Firsts

New Zealand is:

1. The first Western country to conclude a bilateral agreement with China on its accession to the World Trade Organisation (August 1997).
2. The first developed economy to recognise China's status as a market economy (April 2004).
3. The first developed country to enter into Free Trade Agreement (FTA) negotiations with China (announced in November 2004).
4. The first OECD country to sign a high-quality, comprehensive, and balanced FTA with China (April 2008).

(Source: New Zealand Ministry of Foreign Affairs and Trade)

Ambassador Tony Browne, Chair of the New Zealand Contemporary China Research Centre, addresses the Wellington symposium.

New demands, new issues

If we have dropped the ball, or made mistakes if you like – if we have found it hard to keep up with all the demands upon us, I think we must think of that in the context of what has happened in the last 40 years. And that's what I want to sketch out very briefly yet again. Everyone has spoken about the extraordinary changes. I myself went to work in China for the first time at Zhongshan University in 1977, struggled trying to understand concepts like taking class struggle as the key link and the stinking ninth category, but the drama of the change is the first thing I want to dwell upon. The drama of the change since then has left us all behind. And it's not just us here in New Zealand but much of the rest of the world. I mean, we are all looking at a country that has developed an economy from the size of, say, Spain to the second largest in the world, and one that is likely to be the largest by any accounting measure within the next 10 to 20 years. That is a really extraordinary change, and it's been very difficult for everyone to keep up with the new demands, the new issues, that that change gives rise to.

The drama of the change has left us all behind

The second thing, I think, that is worth mentioning – and here I don't think we've lost any ground at all – I think we've built up excellent working relations through the regional architecture that's already been referred to. And we've been helped also by China's own view, famously expounded by Mr Deng Xiaoping as tao guang yang hui – hiding your light under a bushel, taking it quietly – I think the second thing that is very striking is that the development in the last 40 years has been so peaceful. With the exception of one military conflict of note, that is to say the China–Vietnam war of 1979, which was essentially an offspring of the Cold War at the time, China's rise so far has been marked by extraordinary stability and peace. Internally, too, China has suffered only one significant crisis of confidence, namely the one that occurred around the time of the Tiananmen crisis in 1989. But again, China so far has managed to avoid many of the pitfalls and dangers that this dramatically quick and extensive and global development could bring about.

The third issue is China's regional and global perspectives. And we've seen once again recently, in the writings and comments of people like Wang Jisi, how within China there is still an uneasiness, a suspicion, about the United States in particular within the region, which remains the dominant power and with which we have close relations – better and closer relations than we had 10 years ago. That is the challenge for all concerned and I think Phil Goff just referred to the potential tensions and that's something that everyone has to bear in mind. In that context it's also worth mentioning something less tangible, which is a distinct change of mood that has occurred since the global financial crisis, in the sense that there's now a confidence and strength of purpose in China, which has been born of the crisis to some extent, and born to a greater extent of China's own development.

All this is taking place at an extraordinarily important juncture. Not only are we facing a whole spectrum of challenges relating to China's extraordinary growth, but China itself is about to undergo a significant leadership change and the challenges and difficulties facing Mr Xi Jinping and Mr Li Keqiang and others, assuming that they are in due course appointed, are unprecedented and were sketched out, I think extremely interestingly, in the recent report published by the State Council Development Research Centre, the Ministry of Finance, and the World Bank. The report is entitled China 2030 and does underline the enormous challenges facing China today. I could sum up by saying there haven't been any major pitfalls or shortcomings in what we've done, but like everyone, we're facing extraordinary challenges now and in the future.

—*Peter Harris*

Hon. Joe Walding and Chinese Minister of Overseas Trade Bai Xiangguo sign the first trade agreement between New Zealand and China, 9 October 1973.

I would like to suggest four home truths that seem to me to have emerged from where we have got to so far.

The **first** is that while New Zealand's knowledge of China is 100 times better than when we established relations, it is still not enough. This is no longer a peripheral relationship – it is one that is assuming the same sort of importance as those we have enjoyed with Britain, with the United States, with Australia. The difference is that in all those cases we started from a common base – a shared history, shared culture, shared social attitudes, a shared language. As far as China's concerned, most New Zealanders don't have any of those in common. I'm not talking just about the foreign policy elite, but all New Zealanders. Foreign policy can't operate too far ahead of public opinion. Without building our knowledge and our understanding of China, we can't hope to maximise the relationship.

The **second** is that it's a mistake to think that we can have just a transactional relationship. It has to be across the board. A good commercial relationship has to be built on the back of a good political relationship, and both need to be supported by contacts in all the many ways that people and nations relate to one another.

The **third** is that it's a mistake to believe that New Zealand has a special relationship with China, or at least a relationship that is in any way more special than those of the many other countries that believe they have a special relationship. But we do have special attributes that we can bring to the relationship and make work to our advantage. We're small, independent, we have a relatively quick decision-making process, not too many special interest groups, a capacity to take decisions without reflecting overmuch on their wider consequences. The difference in scale can work to our advantage. We didn't get to close an FTA with China because our trade was so important to them, for example. We got it because our trade was so unimportant – China could afford to chance its arm, to try out this new approach without fear of major consequences if things went wrong. We need to be innovative and nimble.

Finally the **fourth** home truth is that China's importance is growing not just to New Zealand, but to the world. It has suitors queueing at its door. I think we have a healthy relationship at present, but it's not one we can take for granted – we are going to have to work doubly hard to keep our position.

—*Chris Elder*

PART 2
THE TRADE AND ECONOMIC RELATIONSHIP

The growth in two-way trade

民以食为天

Sustenance is most important to the people

The way we were

My family had a sheep farm. Our wool went to Bradford, was auctioned there, and made into cloth. It was loaded into British ships, and insured with English companies. We put the money into English banks, and used it to buy English cars. It was the same with dairy exports. They were all traded through Tooley Street. Now Tooley Street's deserted.

—*Sir Douglas Kidd*

Significant gains

The significant gains made over the past 40 years in bilateral trade are impressive. To illustrate this, it is worth looking back at trade levels in 1972 when diplomatic relations were established and when, for example, it is estimated that New Zealand exports to China were less than $2 million per annum and our imports from China equally paltry, at least when compared to today's trade receipts.

China is now New Zealand's second largest trading partner. It still amazes me to see how some New Zealanders I meet are so surprised about this fact and also China's remarkable economic growth over the past three decades. To economic historians, this re-emergence of China has been inevitable and, as they remind us, around the time Captain James Cook was getting mixed receptions as he visited New Zealand in the 1700s, here in China, the Emperor Qian Long was halfway through his reign. At that juncture, it is estimated that China accounted for more than 25 per cent of the world's GDP! Today, even with the amazing development we have seen in China, most estimates still have China only accounting for around 18 per cent of the world economy. This would suggest that there is potentially considerable upside in the story around the growth of the Chinese economy. . . .

However, if New Zealand is to realise the goals of the Government's New Zealand Inc China Strategy, it will mean we will need to grapple with a number of challenges.

Chief among these is perhaps the ability of New Zealand companies to leverage the benefits provided by the free trade agreement. New Zealand is still the only OECD country to enjoy an FTA with China and one of NZTE's key challenges is to ensure that companies who are not in the commodity business – such as dairy products and logs – are fit for market.

Too often we see companies come to the China market, woefully underprepared in terms of tested business strategy, undercapitalised, with unsuitable people to conduct the business and often without a product or service that is tailored to China.

New Zealand companies need to be at the top of their game in China because the domestic market here is becoming one of the most challenging in the world. There are a number of factors that contribute to this:

- the China market has become one of the most fought over with companies, multinationals and even governments competing at every level. One key reason for this is that currently China is one of the few markets in the world that is spending and with plenty to spend.
- Chinese buyers are becoming increasingly discerning and are looking for products and services that are tailored to China.
- the regulatory market is becoming more complex, less flexible, more demanding and less transparent than ever before. One could argue that this is partly a response to protect domestic interests but it is also a genuine attempt by the Chinese Government to ensure that imports of goods and services meet high standards.
- China's own domestic corporate capability has seen dramatic improvements in recent years and on many fronts is able to compete domestically and internationally with all comers. One only needs to think of the success in the ICT sector of Huawei and ZTE to illustrate this.

So in order to capture the undoubted prospects that are present in China, New Zealand companies will need to develop smart business strategies that will allow them to flourish in this increasingly complex market. A key need will be to plan for long-term engagement with established Chinese counterparts by building qualified teams that include in-house Chinese business and Chinese language capability. This latter aspect is in my view one key reason why New Zealand firms struggle to gain traction in this market; they often struggle at the first hurdle because the quality of their business communication is hampered. This could be relatively quickly ameliorated if an appropriate focus on the teaching of Mandarin in New Zealand schools was developed

In the meantime, there is another resource that has been poorly utilised by New Zealand companies to help overcome this issue. Here I am referring to the 300,000 plus Chinese students that have graduated from our institutions over the years, most of whom have had positive New Zealand experiences and who, with their business linkages back in the homeland, could be valuable resources for New Zealand companies as they build their China market capability.

Much too will depend on ongoing growth in the Chinese economy. Certainly most observers expect that the incoming Chinese leadership will need to consider a reduction in fixed asset capital investment so as to boost real productivity to maintain economic growth at levels seen in recent years. But it is a fair bet that while growth rates in China's more wealthy provinces and municipalities (such as Beijing, Shanghai and Zhejiang) may well reduce in coming years, growth rates in other poorer parts of China still have much scope to grow rapidly – this combination of factors should ensure that commercial and investment opportunities in this vast country will continue to be available to smart New Zealand firms who work in tandem with their Chinese counterparts in order to meet the demands of the market.

Simply put, both countries are well placed to build on the significant progress made in the development of the trade economic and investment relationship over the past 40 years.

—Alan Young

Vice Premier Wan Li attends a sheep-shearing demonstration during his 1986 visit to New Zealand. (Photo: Christchurch Press).

Truly remarkable growth

In April next year, New Zealand and China will celebrate the fifth anniversary of the signing of a free trade agreement. I don't think that back when we signed we would necessarily have expected still to be in this position as we approach the first anniversary, but the fact is, New Zealand continues to be the only developed country to have concluded an FTA with China. We are enormously proud of this accomplishment, and what it has meant for our bilateral relationship.

The period under the FTA has seen truly remarkable growth of trade and economic cooperation. Both countries have done well, and the growth rate of New Zealand exports has been particularly spectacular off the lower starting base.

During the four years since the signing of the FTA, New Zealand has exported more to China than during the entire preceding 20 years. The respective totals were $19.2 billion for the four years from 1 July 2008 to 30 June 2012, and $18.7 billion for the 20 years from 1 July 1988 to 30 June 2008.

New Zealand's imports from China during these four years under the FTA have totalled close to $28 billion, making a two-way total trade flow of almost $47 billion. That is a big number to a New Zealand ear.

It is noteworthy that the trade surplus in China's favour has fallen significantly during the FTA era from around 45 per cent of two-way trade during the four years preceding the FTA, to under 20 per cent during the four years under the FTA and to only 11 per cent in the latest trade year to June 2012. Trade has been growing in both directions and also coming into a healthy balance.

China is New Zealand's second largest export market, our number one source of imported goods, and second only to Australia as overall two-way trade partner.

As we near the end of the 40th anniversary year, China is New Zealand's second largest export market, our number one source of imported goods, and second only to Australia as overall two-way trade partner.

Our countries are on track to achieve the goals set by Prime Minister John Key and Premier Wen Jiabao in July 2010 to double trade to $20 billion by 2015.

On current trajectory, by April next year, it should be possible to say that New Zealand's exports to China during the first five years of the FTA exceeded all New Zealand's exports to China in the entire previous history of bilateral dealings, or at least as far back as records go. That is a good mark of the recent acceleration in the pace of development of the New Zealand China relationship. It also points to the prospect of even more remarkable developments ahead if we all do our work well

—*Carl Worker*

A whole new sphere

Ninety-one per cent of our exports to China are commodities – milk powder and logs in particular. That's what we produce well – that was always going to be inevitable. But the future can't be just about those things. Yes, sure, there'll be continuing demands in a world short of those sorts of products. But we only have to look at other small countries around the world that have done better than us economically to know that a country that relies solely on commodities is a country that slips back in the table of nations in terms of wealth and development.

We have to move into a whole new sphere, which I think is around high-value goods and they may be developments of commodities. We've seen what's happened with wine in China and there's probably a market of about 19–20 million people that consume regularly imported wine and we can sell at good prices. We can think about infant formula which is value-added in that way. But we've got to go way beyond that. And what gives me confidence is when I can see companies like Orion Health that are high-tech working in the area of health, and Lanzatech, the company that's taking the waste gas out of steel plants, which is at the top level of environmental technology. And, you know, we can do those things in New Zealand and we need to do those things in New Zealand if we're to be more to China in the long run, than what we were for too many years to the United Kingdom – simply the farmyard for another bigger state. So more in specialised manufacturing, more in the knowledge economy, more in value-added.

Do we have to run fast to stand still? Probably we do.

Have we been making enough progress in the trade relationship? Do we have to run fast to stand still?

Probably we do. But I think you can't possibly doubt the enormous progress that New Zealand has made over that 40-year period of time, from $1.7 million of trade in 1972 to something close to $14 billion worth of two-way trade now. And there are two things, I think, in my political career that have been important in that relationship.

The first was a very straightforward, tiny little amendment to the Education Act in 1989 that said that our school and tertiary institutions could take fee-paying international students. That brought an enormous amount of flak from some New Zealanders who thought it might undermine our education system. In fact, it's now become a $2 billion industry and $600 million of that is Chinese students. And the importance of that is not simply the money. It's all those relationships. I think 300,000 Chinese students have come to study in New Zealand. What better way to develop people-to-people relationships than what we've done there. We've made mistakes, we've stumbled at times, we needed better pastoral care. I think we've learnt from those mistakes.

The second thing is the free trade agreement, and since I signed that agreement in the Great Hall of the People in April 2008 our exports to China have gone from $2.1 billion to $6.2 billion. That's only four years ago that we have trebled our exports to China. And there were some people in this institution that said this is exactly the wrong thing to do and voted against it. Labour and National, the two major parties, saw the potential of that trade agreement and I think we're realising it now. I saw a wonderful article in the Sunday Star Times two weeks ago, where an Australian trader in fruit juice said, this is terrible, I'm paying 35 per cent duty on sending my exports from Australia and here I am competing with New Zealand who's paying no duty. And my Chinese customers are saying move your operation to New Zealand. Given the imbalance in our power and the strength across the Tasman, I thought that is a sign when New Zealand's got the first running. We are still the only developed country to have that free trade agreement. It opened the door, it didn't mean that businesses would automatically go through. So yes, we've got to keep working at it.

—Hon. Phil Goff

Two years ago I was in China, in Wuhan. We went to the largest washing machine factory in the world, the White Swan washing machine factory. And they'd just put in a new production line and I was starting to think, you know, how can Fisher and Paykel ever, ever compete with this sort of scale? And then I noticed a brass plaque on the end of the production line and it said "Made by Scott Technology, Dunedin, New Zealand".

—Hon. Phil Goff

A sustainable relationship

Commodities still dominate our trade with China. However, they are not as dominant as they used to be. As I understand it, last year we exported about $2.5 billion worth of non-commodity products to China. Although that is still not particularly large, it is still important because in 2005 our exports to China were worth about $2.5 or $3 billion. So our non-commodity exports to China have grown substantially. And that is a trend. That is what I have been communicating with Honourable Tim Groser and he has been focussing on this particular issue. That is, we try to export more to China. Of course, we still help Fonterra and all these companies continuously but at the same time we pay attention to high-tech products, as Hon. Phil Goff mentioned. Lanzatech technology in Bao Steel and now in Shougan Capital Steel – they are doing very well. We have a deal between Huawei and Rankin technology. These are the products we are trying to export to China. There is great potential there. And we have talent in New Zealand, indeed, for high technology. So on the one hand we believe that commodity trade is important, but at the same time we are focussing on non-commodity trade and we have great potential there.

But more important than that, I believe, what we need to focus on is not only trade. Trade is very important for us. And at this stage our vision for China is dominated by our economic relations. But at the same time we need strength in our social, cultural, political relations. The social relationship has been growing because we have more and more immigrants, for example. Culturally we have more cultural visitors, delegations visiting China. But we need to have a more comprehensive strategy to enhance our cultural exchanges with China, which will, in the end, help the public to a better understanding of China. That will lay a foundation for a sustainable relationship.

—Dr Jian Yang

The Sale of Services

Tourism The number of Chinese who visited New Zealand in the year to July was ahead 30 per cent from the previous year with those specifically coming for a holiday ahead 38 per cent. Total outward tourist numbers from China in the first half of 2012 were ahead 20 per cent from the same period of a year earlier. So New Zealand is gaining visitors faster than other destinations on average. Some 201,000 visitors from China and Hong Kong in the year to June accounted for $600mn or 10.7 per cent of tourist spending in NZ of $5.6bn.

Education

The number of Chinese students studying in universities overseas rose by 20% in 2011 to reach 340,000, which was a 100% rise from 2007. In New Zealand last year there were 6,199 Chinese students at universities, a rise of 5.7%.

Over 2011 23,071 students from China including Hong Kong studied in New Zealand at all types of institutions. This represented 23.7% of all foreign students compared with 21.6% over 2010 and 22.2% over 2009. However this total is well down from 56,000 in 2003 when China accounted for 46% of all foreign students in the country.

There is no official measure of the contribution of education exports to the NZ economy beyond an Infometrics report of 2008, which estimated a benefit of $2.7bn. Roughly updated to 2011 we estimate education of Chinese in New Zealand contributes between $760mn and $1.2bn in export receipts. The range arises because although Chinese students accounted for nearly 24% of all foreigners studying in New Zealand, Chinese students accounted for 37% of all tuition fee income over 2011, amounting to some $269m of the $732mn total.

—Tony Alexander

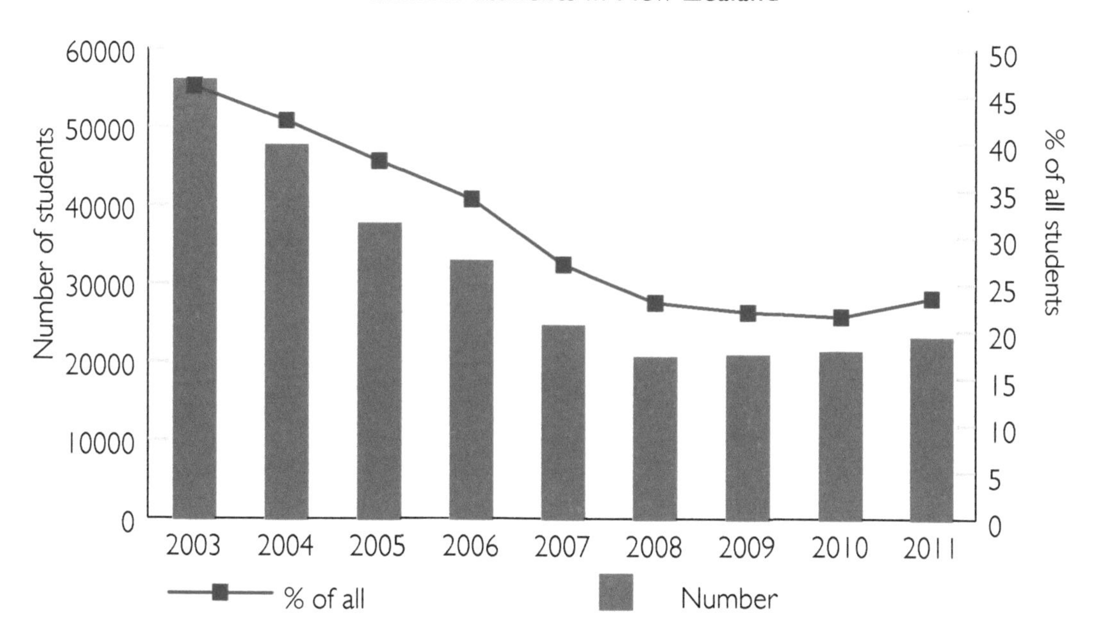

Education New Zealand

Education is an area where we haven't actually got it right all the time. I am in possession of a video that I took in 1992 from the second storey of the Embassy in Beijing of a group of protesters who had refused to allow us to leave the Embassy. That evening they actually got so heated that they broke down the gates and got into the grounds and were forced out by the authorities.

This was not that long after the Tiananmen problems, and protests were supposed to be illegal in Beijing, but this one was a sanctioned protest. We were being sent a very strong message from the Chinese authorities about us getting it wrong. We eventually sorted it out and the students that had been affected got compensation, but it is an example of the boom/bust nature of the education relationship with China which we have to learn from.

We must be doing some things right because China is now our major market for international education. Right now we have about 24,000 students from China studying in New Zealand, but that is lower than some of the peaks. As recently as 2006 we had closer to 40,000 students studying in New Zealand.

What we have to do – and this is a large part of what Education New Zealand will be doing – is try to grow that number, but in a very sustainable way. We're going to have to be much more sophisticated in the way we're promoting New Zealand in the China market, we're going to have to be selling a message that it's not just one way. We have to be much more active actually inside the China market, and I'm very pleased that there are a number of educational institutions talking about serious investment in China. We have to look after Chinese students better than we have before, and we have to stay in touch with those students in a much better way than we have before – there's a huge resource out there that is largely untapped, of Chinese students who have studied in New Zealand. And we have to encourage some of the better students to stay in New Zealand, because that's an absolutely fantastic resource for us. I'm constantly frustrated that our own students aren't integrating more with the Chinese students studying in New Zealand.

Education New Zealand is a new Crown Agency. We've got much more money than we've had in the past, we're coordinated activities across the economy in a way that hasn't been done in the past. Expect to see a transformation in what we're doing in China. We're going to have more people on the ground in different places, and we're going to be very innovative about how we promote New Zealand in the market. For instance,we're working with a documentary film-maker on an approach to trying to sell New Zealand to the parents of Chinese students, and we're looking at a whole lot of web-based activity to make it more exciting for people to think about studying in New Zealand.

—Charles Finny

The view from the sharp end

熟能生巧

Skill comes from practice

Natural History New Zealand

I am at heart a story teller, a documentary maker, an observer;

These are a few of my observations about New Zealand's and NHNZ's journey in China over the past 15 or so years as we traversed the intersection of culture and business.

Why China and what did we hope to achieve?

China was emerging as a superpower and the world was by and large ignorant about China, apart from business or political news reporting.

Our goal was to, in some small way, change that and play a role in bringing China to the world.

For me there were two important and interconnected priorities:

Firstly, we needed to understand China, especially the Chinese mind and culture, and secondly we needed to build relationships based on trust and respect.

From my experience in other parts of Asia I knew that such relationships were not only the key to doing business but also the very foundation on which our aspirations would stand.

We began with SARFT (the State Administration for Radio, Film and Television), SCIO and CCTV.

The first time I met SARFT they said "Very nice to meet you, thank you, goodbye". The second time, "Very nice to meet you, thank you, goodbye". Third time, fourth time, fifth time. The fifth time they said, "What do you want?" I said, "I just want to understand", and they said, "That's good".

And later, they became very good friends, and they said many people came and talked a lot, then left and were never seen again. So they were really looking for commitment. I also built strong relations with the State Council Information Office, China Central Television, and a great many other organisations in China.

We were patient – extremely patient; it took years to establish solid and fertile relationships, but through these we have gained preferential access to both people and places so far denied to our competitors.

Extremely importantly these relationships were two-way – we also looked at what we could give to China,

- We could give China access to the international television market.
- And we could give our expertise.
- Chinese documentary makers had and continue to have a strong desire to

understand western styles of documentary film-making, we have run workshops and given lectures across China and hosted many documentary makers to NZ.

- This was skill transfer.
- We have given a great deal of time to hosting visitors both in our country and in our home; my wife Peggy now has a Chinese brother and I am a New Zealand father to a number of young film-makers.

We made the decision to only work in partnerships and co-productions.

The alternative was to buy our way in on a project-by-project basis, a form of cultural hit and run that is both expensive and unsustainable, a technique favoured by some European and American companies.

We needed two things, **access** and **investment**.

We have succeeded in both those areas.

We are without question the largest non-Chinese producer of documentaries about China in the world.

We have attracted investments in every film we've made and have achieved unparalleled access to parts of China.

We have made over 70 documentaries, which have been screened in a 180 countries around the world with one notable exception: New Zealand.

—*Michael Stedman*

Leveraging the FTA

In the first 20 years I was in New Zealand, China was rarely mentioned. There really wasn't much going on. We always had a great political relationship, but there really wasn't much economics, because what China needed during the late '80s and the '90s when we first developed was markets and capital, and New Zealand was neither in a meaningful way. But today what China needs are good products – we have an emerging consumer population and also a place to invest capital.

On the trade side I would say that we probably haven't leveraged our FTA advantage as much as we could have. I'll give you a simple example. We own a small winery on Waiheke Island, and today our duty for wine into China is zero per cent. For everybody else in the world it's 14 per cent. On top of that you have the luxury consumption tax, on top of that you have VAT. So dollar for dollar for every bottle of New Zealand wine at a minimum we enjoy a 23 per cent advantage versus every other country. Our winery doesn't make 23 per cent either gross or net margin I can assure you. There are very few wineries in New Zealand who make anything close to that.

Ninety per cent of New Zealand wine is white. China at the top is really a red market. Out of the ten per cent New Zealand reds we have some good products, but no one produces in any quantity. Our own little winery produces 11,000 bottles a year – we can't even have a distributor because we don't have enough to distribute.

So what happens is that for us as a country "elaborately transformed" only grew

7 per cent while total exports grew by 134 per cent. So what's wrong with that? Very simple. The vast majority of our businesses are SMEs. There's Fonterra, there's Fisher and Paykel, and then there are SMEs. China is hard even for Fonterra, even for Fisher and Paykel. China is impossible for the small guys. Despite that, a lot of our companies have done very well. But what they need is for us to give them a platform so that they don't have to worry about forming a company, hiring a secretary, finding a distributor, finding office space, finding a lease.

We don't have to market 700 wine brands. I believe it's more than sufficient if we just market Brand New Zealand. Brand New Zealand is a very powerful brand, and most people know New Zealand, think it's safe. It is literally the safest place on earth as far as Chinese people are concerned – it's clean, it's green, it produces great food and beverages.

—*Richard Yan*

Get on and do it

Our story is a little different because we're a new company. We were born on the eve of the global financial crisis, which was a terribly bad piece of timing on my part. In fact, our first shipment of goods out of the processing part of our business went out the week that Lehmans fell over. And we had a plan to attack not just the Chinese market but Southeast Asia and other places in the world as well, with high-value products out of the dairy industry. We found ourselves needing to decide not to do our growth out of debt, but to look for other sources of capital, and we spent a couple of years looking around for the right partner. We ended up focusing on the Chinese market as a source of capital and after talking with several parties over quite a long period of time, bought in about $80 million from Bright Dairy which is part of the Bright Food Group in Shanghai. That allowed us to build further processing capacity, which doubled the size of our operation, and move out of the high-value milk powders we were in and into infant formula.

I actually find doing business in China is pretty much like doing business in any part of the world.

It was a deal that was very easy to do – we did it in two weeks. We found them and we realised that we had very complementary strategies. Actually, we had been courting another party and decided this one looked quite a lot better. And so it gave us some competitive tension and allowed us to do a deal very quickly. But despite the speed with which we did the deal, the relationship has worked fantastically. We got on, we built the plant, and we had our first infant formula product, which we worked in partnership to develop, in the supermarkets in Shanghai within 12 months of doing that deal. And in the first year we'll do about a thousand tonnes of that particular piece of business. They're not our only customer – in fact, they're one of our smaller customers in the Chinese market. They encourage us to work with others. We do that all from here – we don't really use their distribution channels.

And so to return to where I started, I find it interesting when I hear people talking about the challenges of working in China and so forth. Maybe we were just lucky. But certainly, from my point of view, I actually find doing business in China is pretty much like doing business in any part of the world. You find firms that want what you've got, and then you get to know the people and you look for opportunities where we can do simple things better than anyone else, that are of real value to them. And by value I mean that they are prepared to pay plenty for it. And then you get on and you do it. And you do what you say you're going to do. And lo and behold, they ask you to do something else. So, to me it doesn't have some of the mystique that perhaps those who have been around for 40 years find. I find it a very easy place to do business. In fact, the China that I know is an easier part of the world to do business than several of the other countries that we work in.

—*John Penno*

Māori-owned organisations

When I arrived at the Māori Trust I saw there was a huge opportunity to provide a platform to enable Māori to collaborate. We have a vision, which is to mobilise Māori land and assets to create this generation's legacy. One of the things that I observed when working and leading an Iwi organisation – also being the Chair of one of the largest Māori dairy producers, PKW in Taranaki – was that collaboration was required among Māori to truly succeed in business and to provide wealth generation for our people.

In my capacity as Māori Trustee I've had the opportunity to visit China with the Minister of Māori Affairs, and that of course was about bringing together those of our people who are currently running Māori businesses. If you look at the Māori economy and you put that in context, we in New Zealand are a nation that produces food. The natural resources that will be producing that food will in the future come from Māori-owned land and assets. If you look at the current landscape, 37 per cent of the New Zealand fishing industry is owned by Māori. We're participating at present, by virtue of the fact we have Aotearoa Fisheries Ltd, a wholly Māori-owned fishing company. We currently sell product direct to China, predominantly paua and lobster, which is high-value product. One of the challenges with our fishing business is that most of our product currently passes through a particular channel, and we need to ensure that we can capture greater value – not only maintain our margins but also increase our margins over time – by having a presence in China itself, and having some further control in the supply chain.

If you look at the forestry sector, of course, with the CNI settlement under the Labour government 186,000 hectares – the largest forestry estate in New Zealand – is now owned by Māori. Māori own 36 per cent of New Zealand's forestry land. We don't own the trees. And we're not currently actively participating in an integrated value chain and supply chain. However, increasingly Māori want to be more market-facing. We have aspirations to be participating not only as the resource owner but also capturing value at the market end.

In terms of my role as Māori Trustee we've facilitated conversations with potential Chinese partners who can provide not only capital but also opportunities for our Māori-owned organisations to collaborate and get a deeper understanding about what those opportunities might be, not only here in New Zealand but also in China. A recent example was when we were on the delegation with the Minister of Māori Affairs in China we had the opportunity to visit Shanghai Pengxin sheep farm on Chongming Island and to sit down with Chairman Jiang of Shanghai Pengxin to discuss their intentions here in New Zealand. That also provided an opportunity for us to host the Chairman and his people here in New Zealand, which we did last month for a week.

That particular visit was one where we facilitated a meeting where we invited Iwi leaders and chairs of Māori economic authorities throughout the country to come together to have a discussion with the Chairman about what his intentions are here in New Zealand, to deepen the relationship and to also get an understanding of how we might work together, not only here in New Zealand but also in China. Māori of course are not homogenous in our views – there are sections of Māoridom who may not be too pleased with what's happening there. But it's fair to say that those who attended the hui – there were about 25 to 30 and these included major Iwi leaders – were very comfortable with the conversation that was had, welcomed foreign investment in New Zealand and also welcomed the opportunity to partner, in order to provide wealth for our people. That conversation is ongoing.

—*Jamie Tuuta*

Branding in China

"It's a very good question how you position brand when you have a major Chinese partner and they're taking a product and trying to make their own brand. In fact, brand is one of the things you need to think about when you're thinking value. It is a tool, and from our point of view as a New Zealand company with Chinese shareholders, a couple of things. We made very sure that in the founding documents that there wasn't the ability for the parent to pull intellectual property out of the New Zealand company and just take it and use it for themselves. And that any transactions that went on between the parent and the New Zealand company were done at completely arm's length, to the extent that the New Zealand shareholder gets to sign off on those individually and to make sure that there's not leakage of value to the parent. We're a B to B business at this stage, so we look for partners with strong brand presence and that's how we're growing our business. That's not to say we don't seek brand value in those B to B relationships – we do. Everything you do is built into your brand, for better or for worse. And the more you can do to make your brand stronger, and effectively make your company or product something that other people really want, so you have a longer list of customers than you do supply of your product, you can build brand value.

Personally, when we think about the Chinese market, we see ourselves as a small company. We've reached $400 million revenue, but in the Chinese market we are tiny. We just don't believe it's possible that we could establish a brand in that market on our own at this stage in our development. Now, how do we protect our brand? Number one, I don't tend to think about Bright as a Chinese company, they're just one of our partners, and we chose to work with them because they had values that lined up with our own. All companies have got good and bad in their records. But it's not so much what happens to those companies, it's how they respond to those things. And I feel quite comfortable about the way that Bright responds to the issues and challenges that they have in the market. And then physically, we do things like only allowing our name to be associated with products that are made and packed and sealed here in New Zealand, and go in their final form to the market."

—John Penno

"The starting point is really the question of whether there's merit in having a national brand – some sort of halo brand, which would serve as a platform for a range of individual products. Should that be in place for all the countries that we export to? I know there's been a lot of discussion about the New Zealand story, which has been led by New Zealand Trade and Enterprise and Tourism New Zealand. Both John and I were at Stamford two weeks ago and this issue came up in discussions there about nation branding and product branding and where New Zealand sits in the OECD. We had Simon Anholt, who is a world-class leader in this area, stating that New Zealand is now number 13, and he described certain attributes or perceptions of the New Zealand brand. It's always a very young country, clean, green, those

John Penno speaks as a member of the panel addressing economic relations.

particular things. And then we had a discussion about whether that was the case. How clean and green are we? How safe is our food? The conclusion that we drew in the States was that whatever the brand is, we need to say what we do and it needs to reflect what is actually happening on the ground.

We've had discussions, too, through the visits that we've had in China. From a Māori perspective, if I look at Māori Inc, we've got a platform by way of our protocol and tikanga, providing an opportunity to develop relationships that you might not ordinarily establish by taking a different approach. So I see there's merit in the approach that Māori have, in terms of building relationships. And I guess that's just one part of the brand. Too often here in New Zealand we look at ourselves and say this is what New Zealand is, and this is our brand. But that's very inward-looking, and I think we need to get an understanding of how others, like the Chinese, perceive New Zealand."

—*Jamie Tuuta*

"I take it from a slightly different perspective. I grew up in China and we had no brands. I was a director of Unilever and when they had the first Board meeting ever outside of England or Holland they came to China and they asked the Chinese directors, "What should we do differently in China than we do elsewhere?" And I said to them, "Why don't you use the Unilever brand?" And they looked at me as if I was mad. Now, every Unilever product in the world has the "U", and that started in China. In China they have a roof over it, and the line is, " Where there's home, there's Unilever".

The reason a national brand works in China – I'm not sure it works everywhere, but I'm sure it works in China – is because Chinese people have learned about brands in a very, very, short period of time, and they are bombarded by brands from everywhere in the world. China went from being one of the poorest countries to one of the richest in a very, very short period of time. So you just can't educate all those millions and millions of customers through the normal process where you have two hundred years or a hundred years.

I do think for New Zealand a brand New Zealand is important, particularly now in China, and the message is very simple – authenticity. What Chinese people, particularly in food and beverage, are worried about is fake product. And what we do produce is good. Because of New Zealand House I have found out there is an incredible number of good New Zealand businesses I never heard of. And they're all small. A $20 million food company is a big company in New Zealand, but it doesn't even register in China. So the theory behind it is not as important as the practice. I do think if we had a Brand New Zealand, if we had a central platform, we would sell more products."

—*Richard Yan*

The China–New Zealand Free Trade Agreement

捷足先登

The nimble man gets there first

The Development of China–New Zealand economic and trade relations from a new starting point

On April 7, 2008, China and New Zealand signed the China–New Zealand free trade agreement in Beijing that entered into force on October 1, 2008. The agreement covers trade in goods, services and investment.

The agreement is the first comprehensive FTA that China has ever signed and also the first FTA with a developed country.

Since the implementation of the China New Zealand FTA, customs duties levied on goods trade between the two countries have been decreased step-by-step, the market for trade in services has been opened further, and the investment environment has become more regulated and transparent.

2012 is the 40th anniversary of the establishment of China–New Zealand diplomatic relations. This free trade agreement marks a significant milestone in the relationship between China and New Zealand. So, the economy and trade of two countries is at a new starting point.

Trade in goods between the two countries is expanding, bilateral economic and trade relations are becoming increasingly close. China has now become New Zealand's second largest export market and largest source of imports.

According to the agreement, New Zealand will lift tariffs on all products imported from China before 1 January, 2016; the tariffs on 63.6 per cent of products were already lowered to zero when the agreement came into force in 2008. China will lift the tariffs on about 97.2 per cent of all products imported from New Zealand before 1 January, 2019; the tariffs on 24.3 per cent of products were already lowered to zero when the agreement entered into force in 2008.

Following the financial crisis in 2008, China's imports from New Zealand are greater than its exports to New Zealand. Currently, there is a large trade deficit between China and New Zealand.

There exists a strong complementarity in trade between China and New Zealand. China's exports to New Zealand are mainly composed of manufactured products, while New Zealand exports to China include primary products and food.

The services market has been opened and trade in services expanded. Contracting business and engineering by Chinese enterprises in New Zealand shows an upward trend, but with big fluctuations between different years.

The free trade agreement has deepened the economic and trade relations between China and New Zealand. China has become an important economic partner to

New Zealand. And New Zealand was the first developed country to conclude bilateral negotiations for China's accession to the WTO. New Zealand is the first developed country to start free trade agreement negotiations with China. And now, New Zealand has also become the first developed country to have negotiated a free trade agreement with China. New Zealand is the first country to recognise China's market economy status formally.

Economic complementarity exists between China and New Zealand. The FTA is achieving a mutually beneficial win-win outcome, which can promote regional cooperation. The China New Zealand FTA serves as a model for other countries, and will promote the development of multilateral trading systems.

—Associate Professor Ma Tao

Obsession

Soon after my arrival in Wellington I made many friends. One close friend was a New Zealand trade specialist who gave me a 12-page paper, calling for the establishment of a free trade area between New Zealand and Taiwan. I'm a professional diplomat, and because of my training I was on the alert. I felt concerned. Why have this proposed free trade agreement between New Zealand and Taiwan? My reaction was negative.

I went to my friend and said, "Why not have a free trade agreement between New Zealand and China?". He thought I was crazy, but I became obsessed with the idea. I used to have informal lunches with Tony Browne, and I discussed it with Tony. He offered a sympathetic ear, and I found we had shared views. We believed it was the right thing to do, and we started to act. I sent a cable to Beijing, and Tony made representations in Wellington.

If you identify an opportunity, seize it, and work hard, you can make it a reality.

The ball really started rolling in 2003, when China's new President, Hu Jintao, travelled to Australia and New Zealand on his first overseas visit. Top-level visits create momentum. The New Zealand Government took the opportunity of Hu's visit, and pushed hard. Beijing responded. Negotiations towards an agreement were launched during the Hu visit. After his return five rounds of discussions took place.

The meetings finished in April 2008. Later in 2008 Prime Minister Helen Clark came to Beijing for the signing of China's first FTA. In just five years the basis for trade had been completed reformed. What that shows is that if you identify an opportunity, seize it, and work hard, you can make it a reality.

—Ambassador Chen Mingming

A win-win situation

The abiding memory I've got from the Free Trade Agreement is sitting across the table from Bo Xilai, who was then Minister of Commerce. Bo, through his interpreter, at one point leaned across the table and looked me in the eye and said, "I'm very worried about New Zealand's powerful dairy industry". And I started laughing. And he looked bemused at this and, again through his interpreter, he said, "Minister, what are you laughing about?" I said, "Well, Minister, I'm sitting here representing 4.4 million people and you're sitting there representing 1.3 billion people, and you say you're worried about the impact that we will have on you!"

It was clear that dairy products was the issue that we had to break through to get a comprehensive, high-quality, free trade agreement. And what was really helpful was when Wen Jiabao came here in about 2005. Wen said dairy was not an issue for him. And then he said, "I want to see every Chinese child have a glass of milk each day". To which my response was, "Well, that's fantastic, Premier, but I don't think we can actually provide that level of milk for you". But we were able to feed his comments, and his comments about wanting a high-quality, comprehensive agreement, back into that negotiation. And while the Chinese negotiating team held out, we eventually got there. We had to make compromises on time, so all milk powder tariffs aren't phased out until 2019, and we had to make compromises on a safeguard mechanism.

I want to acknowledge Jim Sutton, who started the whole process going. There's a cabinet paper – the first one signed off by Jim and I – in December 2003 where we were putting real pressure on that getting a free trade agreement was something that we really wanted to do, It was going to be a win-win situation for both countries, but frankly, the benefits for us in terms of export levels were going to be much, much higher. We had a meeting when President Hu was here with Helen Clark. We set up the Trade and Economic Cooperation Framework, which Jim negotiated. And in the process of negotiating that, early in 2004, the Chinese side said, would you like a free trade agreement? Would we like a free trade agreement? We're the fiftieth trading partner to China. They, at that stage, were the fourth to us. And we were behind Australia at the time, and our real worry was that if Australia and others got free trade agreements, we would be competitively disadvantaged. Cabinet made a decision within one week of that offer being made, that we would pull out all the plugs and go for it.

Later that year Charles Finny negotiated the first round. David Walker went on to do the other 14 rounds. And we're not only the first developed country: we're still the only developed country. The point that I'd emphasise is that we've got that window of opportunity, that competitive advantage at the moment, and now is the time to be exploiting that. Because we won't have that forever, and sooner or later others will negotiate the same thing.

—*Hon. Phil Goff*

Premier Li Peng is introduced to New Zealand forestry, November 1988. (Photo: National Archives).

Beyond Milk and Trees: is there more to the post-FTA boom in New Zealand exports to China than just minimally processed primary products?

Export Growth Since 2008

Since the FTA came into effect in October 2008 New Zealand's exports to China including Hong Kong have risen 134% while exports to the rest of the world have grown only 4% and China's imports have grown 52%. China now accounts for 15% of all merchandise trade receipts from 7% in 2008. Therefore substantial outperformance has occurred. But can we conclude that this surge is due to the FTA implementation? While the sheer magnitude of the trade growth differences strongly suggests yes, a second look suggests caution in this conclusion.

First, over the same period of time Australia's exports to China have risen by 129% in the absence of an FTA. Australia's exports are overwhelmingly from the primary sector in the form of iron ore and coal principally. Therefore our surge in primary exports may simply reflect the effects of the same forces which have benefited Australia. So have New Zealand's non-primary exports grown as well?

Level of Processing Breakdown

We can address this question using Level of Processing data compiled and released by Statistics New Zealand. These data by country appear on an annual basis and allow us to compare calendar 2011 with calendar 2008. Using these time periods we find that total exports to China including Hong Kong grew 107% whereas to the rest of the world they grew just 3%. Primary exports grew 124% versus 6%, while manufactured exports rose 14% compared with a 7% fall elsewhere. There is evidence of outperformance of manufactured goods exports but the 14% growth over a three year period is not particularly strong. There was also only 7% growth in elaborately transformed manufactures and in fact almost two-thirds of the total growth in manufacturers comes from a 43% rise in exports of chemicals.

	China+ % growth 2008–11	Rest of World % growth 2008–11
All Goods	107	3
Primary	124	6
Unprocessed primary	104	0.2
Processed primary	148	12
Manufactures	14	-7
Simply transformed	19	-10
Elaborately transformed	7	-5

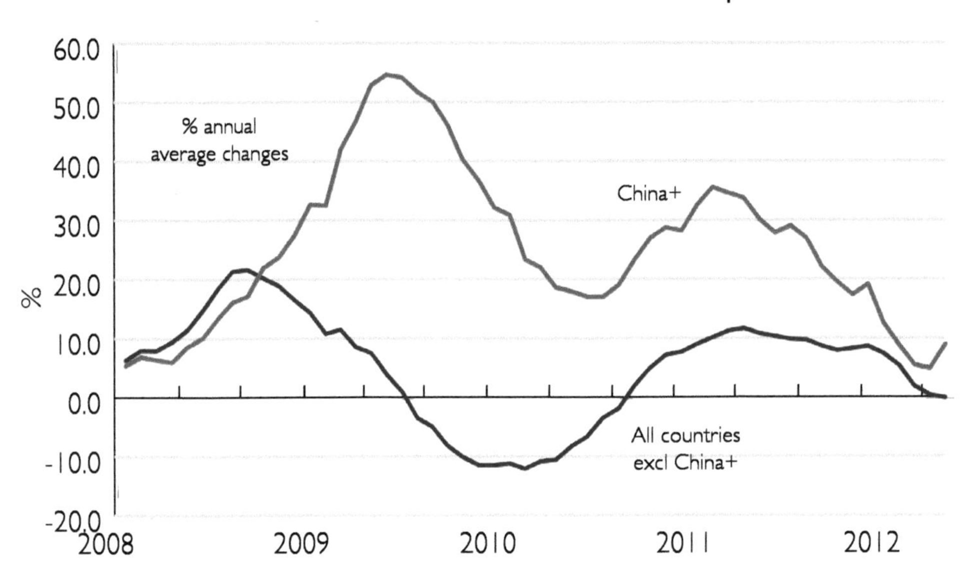

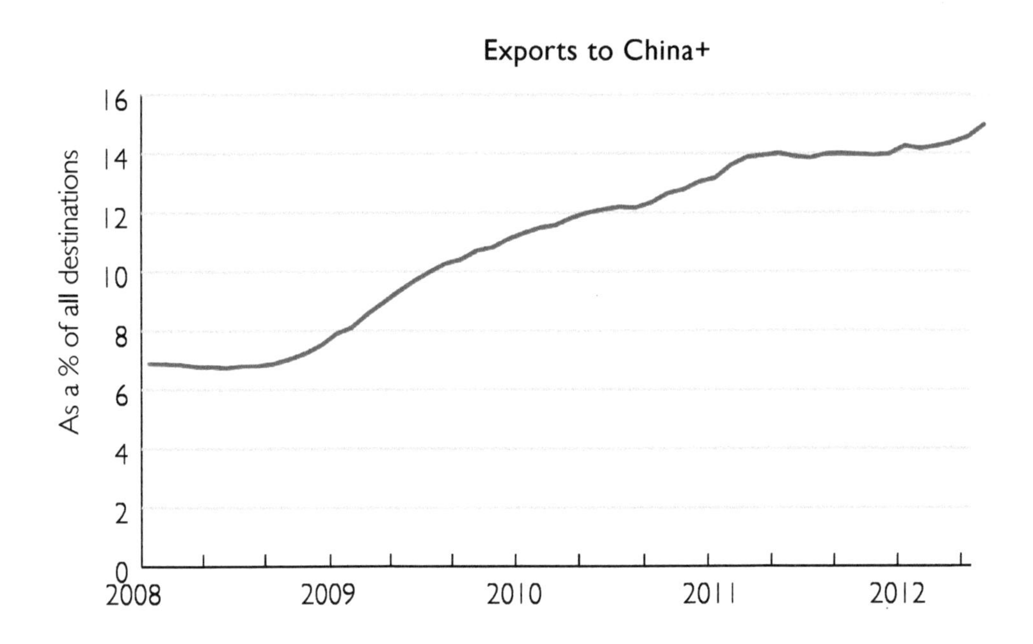

Source: Statistics NZ

We do not have in hand a breakdown of Australia's exports to China for 2008, but using 2009 we find:

total export growth	68%
primary	77%
non-primary	2%

For New Zealand using the same 2011 versus 2009 comparison we find:

total export growth	51%
primary	57%
non-primary	no growth

Therefore, comparing 2011 with 2009 for New Zealand and Australia with China we see that there is no evidence of New Zealand enjoying either especially strong total, primary, or non-primary growth in exports to China. Because Australia does not have an FTA with China it would appear that NZ exporters have not taken advantage of the FTA.

Alternative Breakdown

One area of expertise and comparative advantage for New Zealand is food products processed and packaged for ingredients or final consumption use, with many small operators that we are aware of looking to develop markets for their quality food products. Processed primary exports have risen 148% including a 174% rise in processed food exports.

We can perhaps get a better feel for what is happening if we create an alternative breakdown of exports into primary including basic metals and chemicals etc versus non-primary including largely elaborately transformed manufactures and processed primary including the likes of wine.

Doing this we find that between the year to October 2008 and June 2012 New Zealand's merchandise exports to China including Hong Kong have risen 134%, exports of primary products have grown by 141% and non-primary exports 32%. For the rest of the world these growth rates were -2% and 3%.

Is there evidence that growth in non-primary exports is picking up? Mild but not yet a sustained trend. Primary exports were up by 8% in the year to June while non-primary exports to China were ahead by 17%. This growth divergence is not evident for the rest of the world in that primary receipts from the rest of the world fell by 0.3% in the year to June while non-primary receipts from the rest of the world rose only 0.8%.

Therefore, this past year has produced not only a lift in non-primary export growth to China but also a lift not seen for other parts of the world. This could therefore be an indicator that following the Free Trade Agreement coming into effect in October 2008, New Zealand is benefitting from more than just faster primary sector export growth.

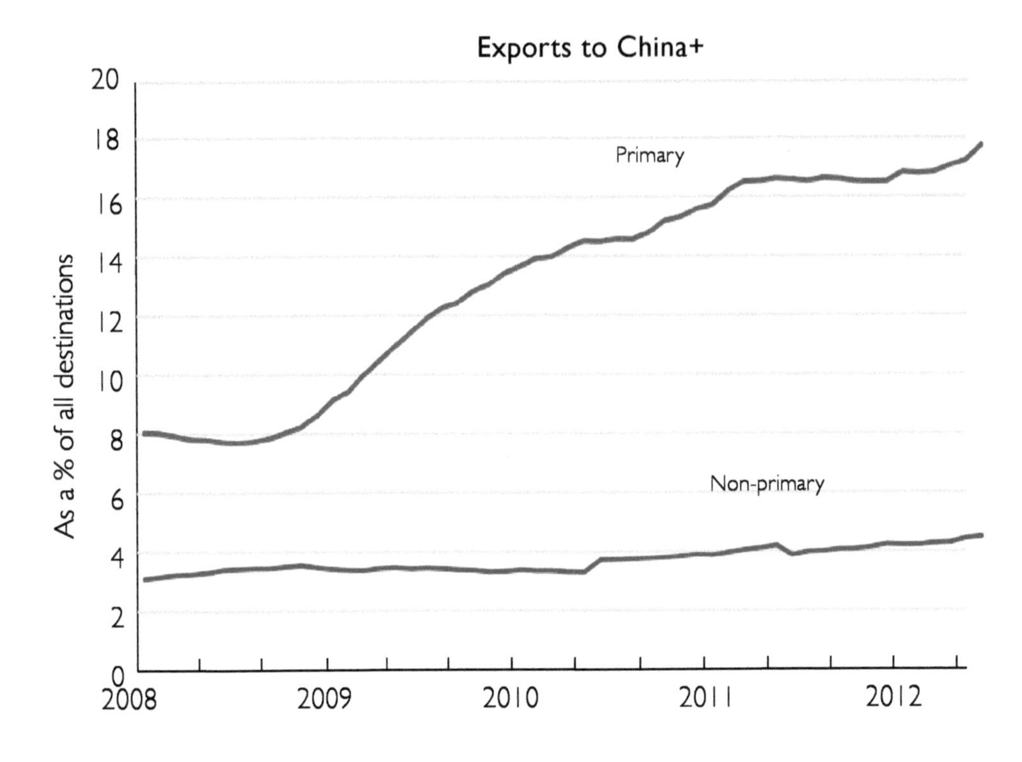

Source: Statistics NZ

Source of Most Recent Growth?

Can we identify where this non-primary growth is coming from?

In the year to June 2012 non-primary exports to China+ totalled $403mn (compared with $6.4bn primary). This was a rise of $59mn from the year to June 2011. The main contributions to this rise came from the following goods categories.

Optical, photographic, cinematographic, measuring, checking, medical or surgical instruments and apparatus; parts and accessories	+116% or $17mn to give $32mn
Glass and glassware	+2,100% or $5mn reaching $5.5mn
Plastics and articles thereof	+5.7% or $1.8mn to reach $33mn
Beverages, spirits and vinegar	+29.4% or $11mn to reach $49mn

The $59mn improvement largely comes from increased exports of what one would guess is wine, along with plastic and glass articles and optical or medical equipment.

Data Conclusion

Based on total export growth of 134% one cannot strongly conclude that the FTA has been effective as:

- Australia's exports have soared by a similar proportion.
- Exports of elaborately transformed manufactures have risen only 7%. However we can cite as evidence of good FTA use a 174% boom in processed food exports. Plus the overall performance is good considering the challenging export environment.
- Fewer than four years have passed from the FTA becoming effective.
- Some items still face tariffs.
- We have experienced the biggest global economic downturn in decades.
- There is reduced availability of credit and business deleveraging.

—*Tony Alexander*

The New Zealand-China Free Trade Agreement

The Free Trade Agreement between New Zealand and China (NZ–China FTA) came into force on 1 October 2008. The NZ–China FTA was signed on 7 April 2008 in Beijing, bringing to an end a negotiation process that had spanned 15 rounds over three years.

The NZ–China FTA is a treaty between New Zealand and China that liberalises and facilitates trade in goods and services, improves the business environment and promotes cooperation between the two countries in a broad range of economic areas.

Liberalised trade in goods

The NZ–China FTA provides for the removal over time of tariffs on 96 per cent of New Zealand exports: New Zealand will make an annual duty saving of $115.5 million, based on current trade.

Rules to govern trade

The NZ–China FTA contains rules to determine which products qualify for tariff cuts (the "Rules of Origin") as well as rules to counter unfair trade or unexpected surges in imported products from the other country.

Liberalised trade in services

The FTA also covers services and New Zealand service providers benefit from China expanding its commitments in services including in education and environmental services.

Movement of people

New Zealand will also benefit from provisions to facilitate the travel of business people to China and from access to skilled workers from China in certain occupations where long term skills shortages exist.

Facilitation for investment

In the area of investment, New Zealand will benefit from enhanced protections for investments established in China, as well as a provision to ensure that New Zealand investors remain competitive with investors from other countries. The FTA also provides New Zealand investors with access to binding third-party arbitration procedures if the Chinese Government breaches the investment provisions.

Measures to improve the business environment

The NZ–China FTA aims in other ways to improve the business environment and open up opportunities for business.

Measures relating to:

- customs procedures
- sanitary and phytosanitary procedures
- technical barriers to trade, and
- intellectual property

are designed to reduce barriers to doing business between New Zealand and China.

The NZ-China FTA establishes a framework for cooperation to enhance the benefits of the FTA. The objective is to build on the existing cooperative relationship and create new opportunities for both countries.

Source: New Zealand Ministry of Foreign Affairs and Trade

The investment conundrum

小钱不去 大钱不来

If small money doesn't go out, big money won't come in

"I think it's been a poorly informed debate, and we have a responsibility to make sure that New Zealanders really understand how important foreign investment is."

—*Sir Graeme Harrison*

"Increasing two-way bilateral investment is critical for maintaining a sustainable economic relationship."

—*Jason Young*

"While it is widely accepted that investment flows between New Zealand and China should more closely reflect broader trade flows including goods and services, the reality has been different."

—*Alan Young*

"China's central Government encourages Chinese enterprises – not only the state owned enterprises but also the private enterprises – to go out and invest abroad. China welcomes transnational companies to invest in China, not only in the coastal regions but also in the central and western regions."

—*Dr Ma Tao*

"By high-quality investment, what we mean is foreign investment that will bring new thinking, technology and management practices into New Zealand businesses, will create sustainable and high-productivity employment, will add to current high-quality investment rather than be a substitute for it, and will create sustainable, high-value-added export opportunities for New Zealand."

—*Girol Karacaoglu*

"We've got no prejudice for or against any investment partner, we just want to see the investment go into areas that add value to New Zealand, and not simply to land prices of farmland that is already overvalued."

—*Phil Goff*

"I'll tell you what, I'd rather have Chinese equity invested in my land than I would have too much debt, and have all that interest going back offshore anyway."

—*John Penno*

"Chinese foreign investment will change the industrial structure and trade relations in the region."

—*Prof. Han Feng*

A major turning point

While it is widely accepted that investment flows between New Zealand and China should more closely reflect broader trade flows including goods and services, the reality has been different. While there have been some solid signs of positive change in the last three to four years, there are still a number of issues to overcome.

One is New Zealanders' savings record. New Zealand's relatively low rate of savings means that New Zealand companies don't have a large pool of capital to invest overseas, including to China.

And neither has the overall history of bilateral investment to date been smooth sailing. CITIC Pacific's investment in New Zealand forestry assets in partnership with Fletcher Challenge in the 1990s was not a success and CITIC withdrew from the market. On the New Zealand side, Lion Nathan invested in breweries in East China in the mid-1990s before pulling out in 2004 with losses exceeding $100 million. More recently, Fonterra's 43 per cent investment in Sanlu was largely written off as a fallout from the melamine scandal. Without going into the causes of the failures, they have cast a shadow over two-way investment. It has only been in the last year or so, for instance, that Chinese companies have shown interest in investing again in forestry assets and processing, this despite log exports being New Zealand's second largest export to China. One notable exception however has been Fonterra. Despite the Sanlu experience, Fonterra was quick to re-engage in the China market, although the recent dairy farm investments have been on the basis of strong controlling stakes.

Official statistics don't accurately capture the real level of foreign direct investment flows. This is due to most Chinese FDI in New Zealand being routed through subsidiaries of mainland companies registered in Hong Kong, Singapore and other tax effective jurisdictions. While the official statistics publicly available are limited, the scale of most FDI investment from China can be found on publicly available sources, as the investments have been into listed companies or have been widely reported in the media – for example Haier investing into Fisher and Paykel, Bright Dairy into Synlait, Agria (including New Hope) into PGG Wrightson and Pengxin into the Crayfar farms. Based on our best estimates by the end of 2012, Chinese FDI in New Zealand is likely to be in the order of NZ$2 billion.

So how does the future bilateral investment picture look? On this 40th anniversary, it is timely to note that we have reached a major turning point in the history of bilateral investment. With New Zealand's investment in China, by far the most significant project underway is Fonterra's announced plan to develop "milk pools" in China, which will involve developing more than 30 farms in China by 2020. To date two farms are in production with a third one coming on stream by the end of this year. The estimated cost of the investment will exceed $1 billion and Fonterra will need to be opening a new farm of 3,000 cows every two to three months to meet the target. To meet part of this capital requirement Fonterra have set up the Fonterra Shareholders Fund, which will allow domestic and foreign shareholders – including Chinese – to participate in Fonterra's growth. The China farm development programme will be a significant beneficiary of this. The Fonterra Shareholders Fund was launched on 30 November to strong support in the market. Overall the Fonterra China investment programme will underpin the continued growth in New Zealand's dairy exports to China with significant transfers of modern dairy technology to the Chinese dairy industry.

On the inbound investment site, the two major developments this year have been Haier's acquisition of Fisher and Paykel appliances at a price which values Fisher and Paykel at close to $1 billion and demonstrates the value that Haier has placed on acquiring New Zealand whiteware technology and international marketing expertise. Secondly and perhaps more significantly, since it is in the agricultural investment area, has been the Shanghai Pengxin settlement on the Crayfar farms last month after a series of legal challenges. The Supreme Court's decision has, in effect, given the green light to a range of major new greenfields investment projects – in the dairy sector in particular – which are likely to be announced in the next few months, with a total investment in the order of $500 million, with further projects in the pipeline. These developments, together with the Haier and Pengxin investments, indicate that New Zealand is clearly on the map as a destination for Chinese investment.

—*Alan Young*

The development of bilateral direct investment

With the deepening of two-way exchanges among enterprises of the two countries, the investment is expanding. Chinese government encourages enterprises to "go out", as an outward investment strategy. Large foreign reserves are helpful for enterprises to invest abroad. China's outward FDI mainly seeks for resources and energy, especially in developing countries. Bilateral investment expands continuously these years (see top figure, p.62), improving the level of economic cooperation.

Chinese enterprises' direct investment in New Zealand increases quickly. In 2008 when the agreement was signed, the direct investment flows to New Zealand increased from -$1.6mn in 2007 to $6.46mn, further increased to $9.02mn in 2009, and jumped to $63.75mn in 2010 (see bottom figure, p.62).

In terms of investment, China and New Zealand promised to give each other's investors treatment not less favourable than its own investors enjoy, and to guarantee that more favourable provisions negotiated by either country in future FTAs with third parties will be extended to the other country.

Meanwhile, the agreement made detailed, clear provisions on investment protection, investor-state dispute settlement procedures and rules, which established an effective mechanism to resolve investment-related disputes.

Here are some examples and cases of Chinese enterprises investing to New Zealand. In 2009, Haier group bought New Zealand's largest household electrical appliance enterprise Fisher and Paykel to get 20 per cent equity, which is

Source: CEIC Data.

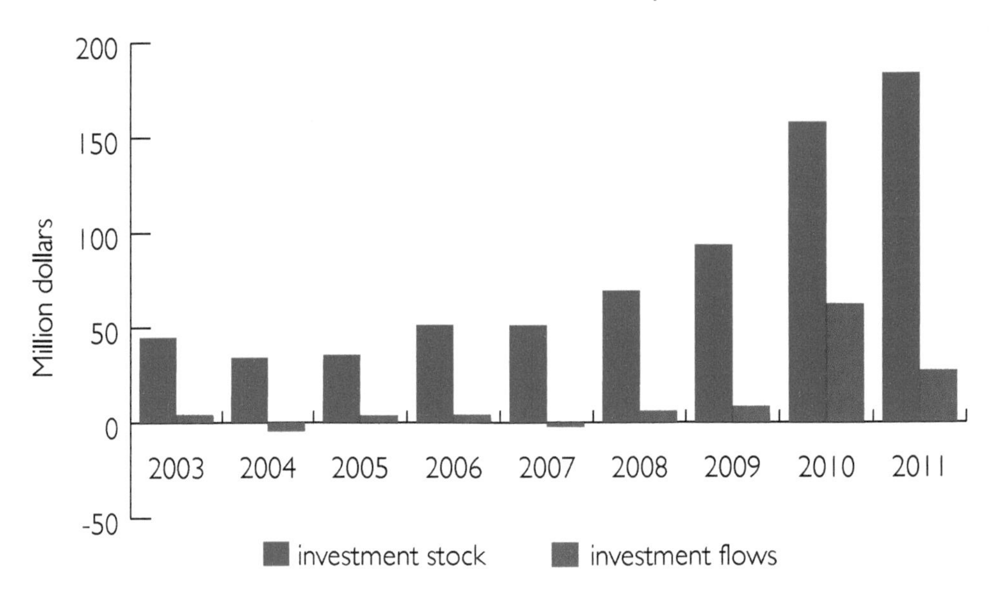

Source: Ministry of Commerce of China.

an example of bilateral cooperation in science and technology.

New Zealand's largest agricultural service corporation PGG Wrightson sold 13 per cent equity to the China's Agria Species Group Co., Ltd. A joint corporation will be established in China to develop agricultural service business.

In 2010, Bright Dairy Company of China won the control equity of Synlait Dairy, which is located in South Island of New Zealand. Synlait is one of the five largest milk-processing enterprises in New Zealand, mainly engaged in milk powder production and processing business. In October of 2010, Bright Dairy bought 51 per cent equity of Synlait.

As Dr Jason Young pointed out in an interview, New Zealand agricultural enterprise can make a direct investment in China, which is a tremendous opportunity for New Zealand agricultural enterprises. Considering the China–New Zealand FTA, New Zealand companies enjoy great advantages in investing in China. So China welcomes more and more New Zealand's enterprises to invest in China, to help China's agricultural and animal husbandry industry obtain greater progress.

—Dr Ma Tao

Investing in the Economic Integration of China and New Zealand

Increasing two-way bilateral investment is critical for maintaining a sustainable economic relationship.

An OECD Science, Technology and Industry Working paper from 1999 conducted a thorough overview of the relationship between investment and international trade. The report took an empirical approach to this question, arguing that the relationship between trade and investment cannot be inferred from a purely theoretical analysis.

Three of the report's findings are important for today's discussions.

First, until the mid-1980s, international trade generated direct investment. After this period, the cause-and-effect relationship seems to have been reversed, with direct investment heavily influencing trade.

Second, evidence indicates that foreign investment abroad stimulates the growth of exports from originating countries (investing countries) and, consequently, that this investment is complementary to trade. Analysis of 14 countries demonstrated that each dollar of outward FDI produces about two dollars' worth of additional exports.

Third, in host countries, short-term foreign investment most often tends to increase imports, whereas an increase in exports appears only in the longer term. However, in the short term, host countries enjoy many benefits from foreign investment (technology transfers, job creation, local subcontracting, etc.).

From this report and the practical experience of many countries, including both China and New Zealand, we can see that there is a strong relationship between trade and investment. More particularly, investment supports the trade relationship both in the short-term and in the long run.

This is important for the NZ–China relationship. Economic relations between China and New Zealand have been going from strength to strength since the establishment of diplomatic relations and in particular since the 2008 Free Trade Agreement came into force.

There has been a steady growth in the share of Chinese imports in the New Zealand market. China became the largest source of New Zealand imports, overtaking Australia this year.

Likewise, China is buying an increasing share of New Zealand exports. This figure shows a particularly large growth in post-FTA years as tariffs were removed and New Zealand exporters began to focus more strongly on the growing Chinese market.

Country of Origin of NZ Imports (% share)

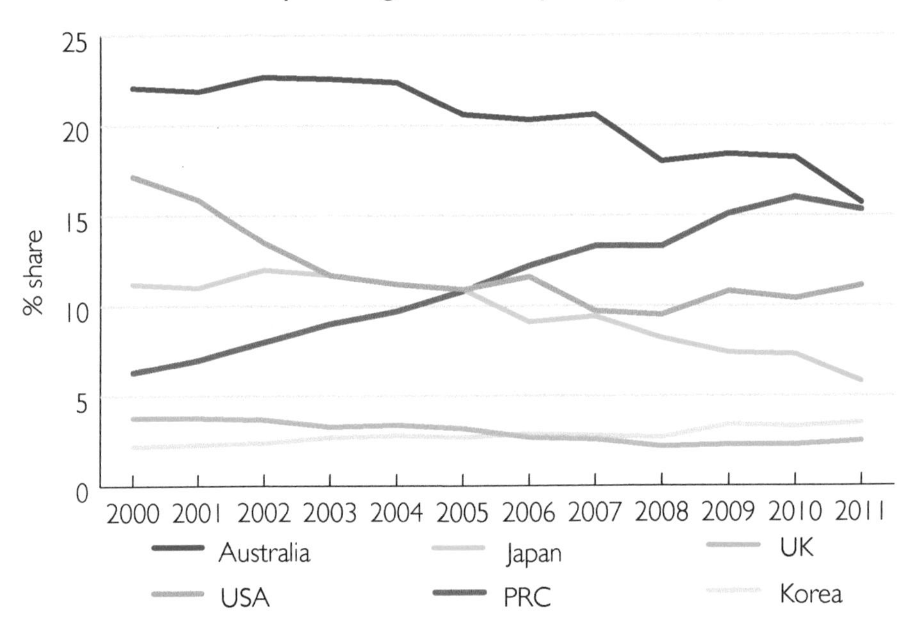

But this rapid growth in the trading relationship has yet to be followed by a rapid growth in the investment relationship. This figure shows the top six trade partners of New Zealand and compares their share of New Zealand imports and exports with their share of investment.

New Zealand's long-time important economic partners, Australia, the UK and the US are all also incredibly important investment partners. Even though their share of both imports and exports has decreased over the last few decades, they remain the main holders of the stock of total investment in New Zealand. They are also the main countries New Zealanders choose to invest in.

Conversely, the PRC, and to a lesser extent Japan and South Korea, represent

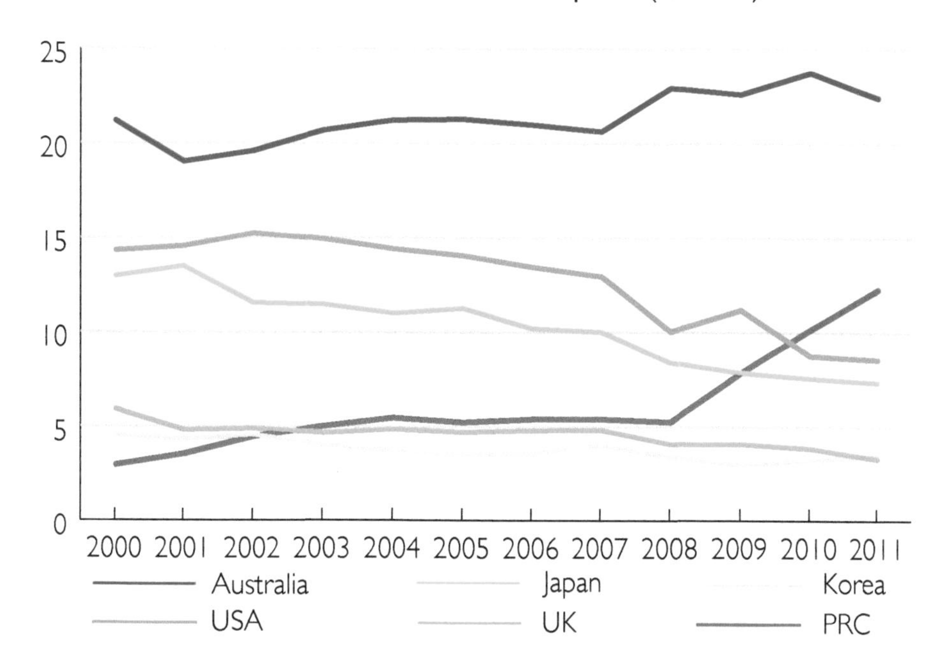
Share of NZ Overseas Trade Exports (% share)
25
20
15
10
5
0
2000 2001 2002 2003 2004 2005 2006 2007 2008 2009 2010 2011
Australia
Japan
Korea
USA
UK
PRC

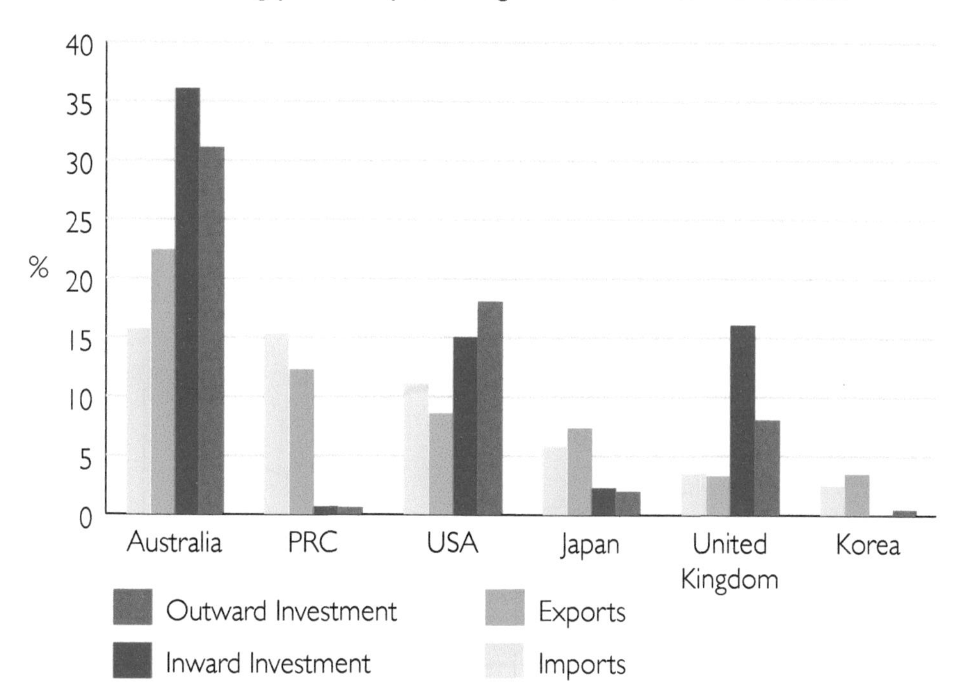
Trading partners percentage share of investment stock
40
35
30
25
%
20
15
10
5
0
Australia
PRC
USA
Japan
United Kingdom
Korea
Outward Investment
Exports
Inward Investment
Imports

a large share of New Zealand trade but a very small share of bilateral investment. Unlike the trade relationship, the investment relationship remains small and has made only modest gains since the FTA came into force.

This figure shows the total investment stock from China in New Zealand and from New Zealand in China. As you can see, to the year ending 31 March 2011, NZ$1.8 billion investment stock from the PRC represented only 0.6 per cent of the total investment stock in New Zealand. Likewise, the NZ$769 million worth of investment stock from New Zealand into China represented only 0.5 per cent of New Zealand's total investment stock abroad.

There have however been modest gains from a very low base. Over the last 10 years Chinese investment in NZ has grown from 0.3 per cent of the total to 0.6 per cent. NZ investment in China has grown from 0.1 per cent of NZ overseas investment to 0.5 per cent.

Investment flows also show an on-going dominance of investment by New Zealanders to our traditional trade partners though China is beginning to feature more. New Zealanders invest the most in the US and Australia.

Likewise, investment flows into New Zealand remain dominated by Australia, the US and the UK.

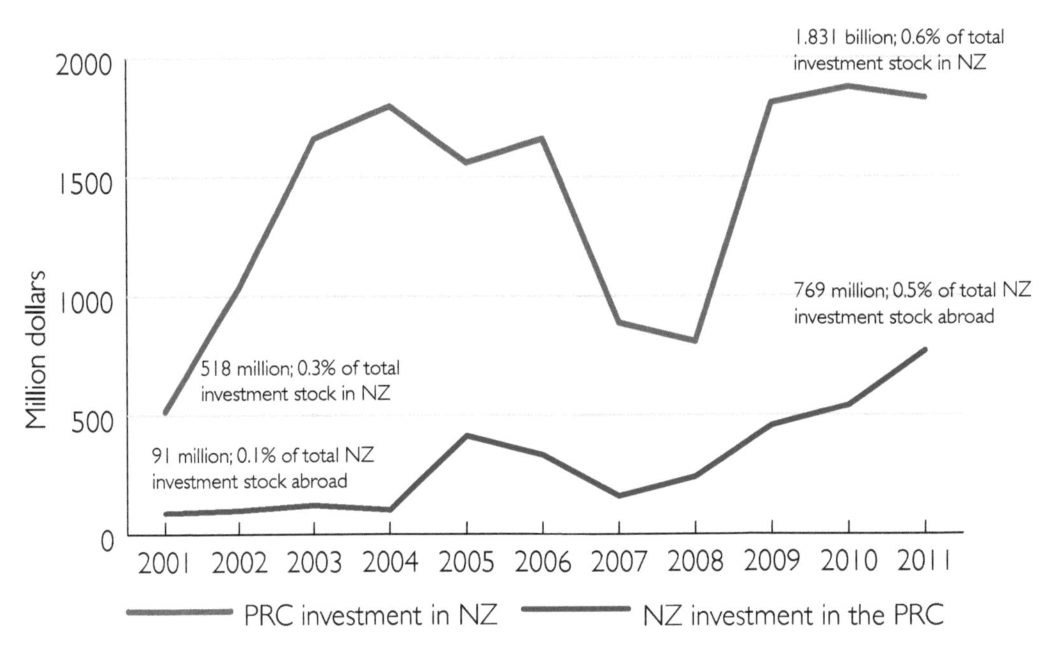

Flow of Total New Zealand Outward Investment to Year-end March 31

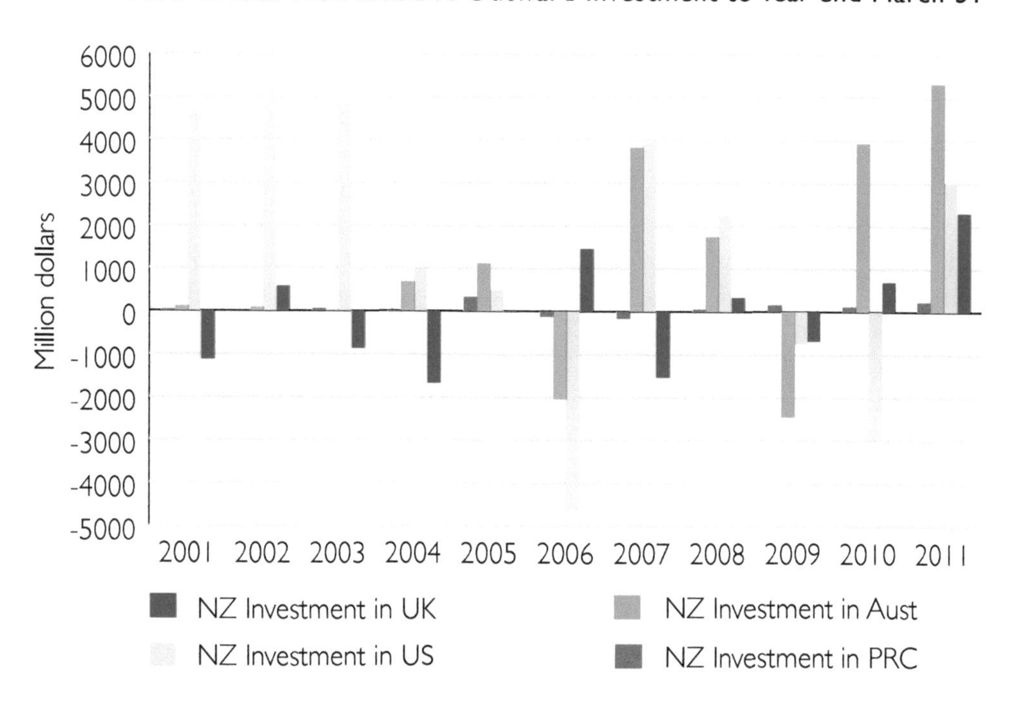

Flow of Total New Zealand Inward Investment to Year-end March 31

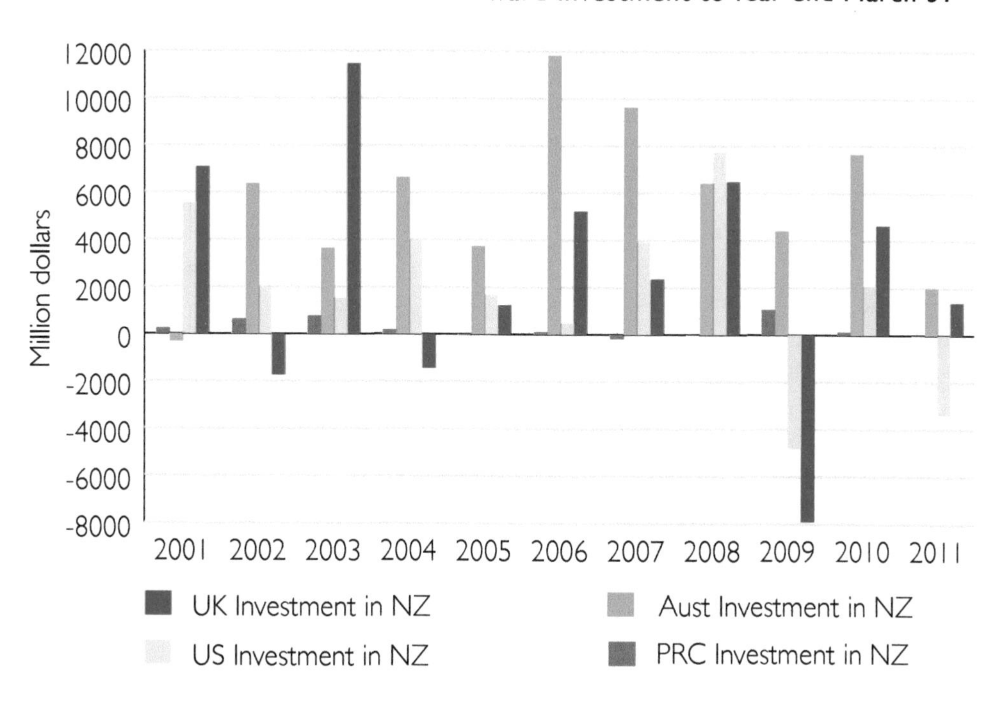

Government Positions

From these statistics we can conclude that the rapid growth in the trading relationship between China and New Zealand has been followed by a more modest and less rapid development of the investment relationship.

However, governments in both countries recognise that a sustainable economic relationship requires the development of bilateral two-way investment.

For example, this quote from Trade Minister Tim Groser acknowledges this challenge.

"Trade and investment are increasingly linked in today's global supply chain. It is inconceivable that this vast expansion of China–NZ trade links would not be accompanied by a major expansion of Chinese investment in New Zealand and vice versa. If you look at the stock of foreign investment in New Zealand it is Australian, British, and US that dominate it. Why? Because these countries have been our major economic partners. This will change in line with the very radical shifts in New Zealand trading partners. It needs to change."

Likewise, in a recent meeting in Phnom Penh, Premier Wen Jiabao said to Prime Minister Key that China is ready to expand its imports from New Zealand and welcomes the country's continuous expansion in the Chinese market. Moreover, Premier Wen called on the two governments to create a better environment for expansion of mutual investment.

This year the New Zealand Government released a comprehensive strategy for promoting an all-round relationship with China. The fourth goal in this strategy is to "Increase bilateral investment to levels that reflect the growing commercial relationship with China."

And both the Ministry of Foreign Affairs and Trade and New Zealand Trade and Enterprise are working hard to build a long-term sustainable investment relationship. There are many examples of pioneering investors in both economies that suggest that over the next few decades the investment relationship will continue to grow to more closely to reflect the growing commercial relationship.

In summary, studies show the relationship between trade and investment is significant. Trade not only increases bilateral investment but also helps sustain and grow the trading relationship.

The New Zealand–China trade relationship has grown rapidly, especially since the signing of the 2008 FTA. However, the investment relationship has grown more slowly. Investment represents a deeper level of economic integration between China and NZ and will take some time to develop. The challenge for the next 40 years of diplomatic relations is to build a sustainable investment relationship to support the strong trading relationship.

—*Jason Young*

Rebalancing trade and investment

Chinese investment abroad has kept increasing in recent years. Two features are: 1) the speed of the inflow of Foreign Direct Investment (FDI) is slower than the outflow (11 per cent versus 17 per cent in 2011); 2) China overtook Japan in 2010 to rank fifth in the world, with total FDI of US$300 billion. It is widely predicted that Chinese FDI will grow more quickly because of the structural readjustment domestically, and the large amount of foreign reserves. Chinese foreign investment will change the industrial structure and trade relations in the region. With a more balanced relationship between Chinese trade and investment, China will be more efficient in carrying out the strategic change necessary for its development, which will be beneficial first to the green and new industries, relating to clean energy, new materials, agriculture, food processing, the dairy industry, as well as the environmental industry and raw material and resource supply.

New Zealand has set its strategy "Opening Doors to China" adapting to this development already, and its current investment in China is mainly in the fields of forestry, agriculture, light industry, textiles, food processing, the metallurgical industry, the medical industry, and the dairy industry.

—Prof. Han Feng

A poorly informed debate

"I think that what we have had is a paucity of public information about foreign investment, and I would urge Treasury, because there is no other body now that is actually able to put out a very well-informed document on the level of foreign investment in New Zealand. It's interesting that a lot of the anti foreign investment comments have come from Auckland, and yet 50 per cent of foreign investment in New Zealand actually goes to Auckland. So I think it's been a poorly informed debate, and we have a responsibility to make sure that New Zealanders really understand how important foreign investment is."

—Sir Graeme Harrison

Cheap capital

I wasn't a greatly experienced person when it came to bringing investment in. I guess my simple rule was that if it was all done here in New Zealand under New Zealand law and the money came to New Zealand then it should be reasonably straightforward. But I suspect that bringing money here and having it invested here in New Zealand companies under New Zealand law feels more straightforward to me than heading the other way with my cash – I'm not sure that I'm ready to do that. But perhaps the Chinese feel the same way about it. They understand their own system, I'm sure, much more readily than they understand ours.

The whole area of Chinese investment in New Zealand amuses me. It's quite strange to think about some of the debate that's gone on in New Zealand over the past two years on a couple of fronts. One, they're such a big trading partner with us, why would we be concerned about their capital coming this way? The reality is they have freely available capital, and therefore it's much cheaper than you can get from this part of the world. Some of you may remember at the time our company was trying to raise capital we actually had an attempt at an IPO in the New Zealand market. The deal that we eventually did was four times better than we could have attracted in the New Zealand market at that time, and that's just a story about the cost of capital.

They're such a big trading partner with us, why would we be concerned about their capital coming this way?

That capital then allowed us to get on, build the business, expand the plant. We had 400 people employed on the job for a year while we were doing the build. It was a sophisticated infant formula plant, most of the people were returning highly trained Kiwis who had gone offshore to find employment in industry.

Even in the case of dairy farmers – should we be selling dairy farms? Well I'll tell you what, I'd rather have Chinese equity invested in my land than I would have too much debt, and have all that interest going back offshore anyway. The dairy industry today has $3.5 billion or thereabouts tied up in debt on farms, and the interest bill on that is about $1.7 billion a year flowing back offshore. We don't debate that anywhere near enough.

—*John Penno*

Adding value

It is a misconception that Labour is against Chinese investment. We negotiated a chapter in the FTA that gave preferential investment to China. We are not against investment from China – in fact investment from China is tiny – $1.8 billion I think. In Australia it's $100 billion. What we were against is the question of investment in farmland. I want to go back to what Girol said, that we need high-quality investment, new thinking, new technology, new management techniques, and we do need all of those things, and because we don't save enough we've got to use other people's savings, but actually of all the areas I'd like to see investment go into, the area I'm least enthusiastic about is farmland, because we've already got the ability there. Ask the Chileans, where we've invested in Kiwi tech in Chile, and we've brought in animal husbandry, pasture management, high-tech agritech. It's doesn't add to that value that you were talking about for us to sell off our farmland and the only reason that Shanghai Pengxin was an issue, and the Germans in Southland were not, was because a guy called Michael Fay took it to court. Labour's view on both is exactly the same. We've got no prejudice for or against either investment partner; we just want to see the investment go into areas that add value to New Zealand, and not simply land prices to farmland, which are already overvalued. Look at the $35 billion of debt – if we get everyone coming in wanting to buy farmland that's going to push farm prices up, it ain't going to improve our productivity.

—*Phil Goff*

High quality investment

The government's business growth agenda rests on six pillars. One is building export markets. Another is building capital markets. The third is encouraging innovation. The fourth is natural resources, then infrastructure, and skilled and safe workplaces. Just focusing on foreign investment in that broad context, New Zealand needs and welcomes foreign investment. It has been part of its economic history, and growth is based on foreign investment. This includes direct investment, both inward and outward. What matters is the quality of that investment.

By high-quality investment, what we mean is foreign investment that will bring new thinking, technology and management practices into New Zealand businesses, will create sustainable and high-productivity employment, will add to current high-quality investment rather than be a substitute for it, and will create sustainable, high-value-added export opportunities for New Zealand. As long as it does all that, it's extremely welcome. It fits with the New Zealand overall economic strategy, and it also fits with the business growth agenda of the government.

As we speak, there is a multi-agency group looking carefully at the actual and perceived obstacles to high-quality investment, and engaging with various people, and we are very happy to engage with anyone to help us identify those obstacles. We are going to actively seek input from all sorts of people, business people included, as well as those people who have serious concerns about foreign investment in New Zealand. We are aware that among these obstacles is a lack of clarity about the rules and regulations applying to foreign investment, and it's our duty to make sure that those are clearly set out.

At the end of the day, the idea is to have an environment that supports the kind of foreign investment that supports New Zealand's overall strategy led by the private sector. We want to support the private sector to get on with its job of creating wealth and economic growth. Within that overall strategy, the New Zealand–China relationship has been identified as a priority relationship, both in terms of the government's New Zealand Inc Strategy and Treasury's priorities. The top three bilateral relationships we've identified are China, the US and Australia.

—*Girol Karacaoglu*

PART 3
THE PEOPLES AND THE CULTURES

The information gap

实事求是

Seek truth from facts

Domestic politics are very important

I'm here to speak about my views on China and New Zealand. Now first of all I might make a very brief observation and that is that New Zealand–China relations can be a domestic issue in New Zealand, but it is unlikely to be a domestic issue in China. Because the Chinese tend to focus on great power relations. My personal experience can explain the development of New Zealand–China relations. In 1972 when relations were established, I was at primary school in China and I'm not sure that I'd really heard of New Zealand. I was in the countryside – my parents were sent to the countryside. They were primary school teachers and they were sent to the countryside during the Cultural Revolution to be re-educated by peasants. That was in 1972. And then in 1980 I studied at university and my degree was in American studies. So New Zealand was not particularly important in those years. I didn't know much about New Zealand. I'd heard about Rewi Alley, of course, a great friend of China. And then in 1994 I went to Australia, to the Australian National University, to do my PhD there. And that was Australia, right, I was moving closer to New Zealand.

In 1972 trade between New Zealand and China was very small – $1.7 million. Exports to China were only $1 million. But then, gradually, the trade started to grow. And of course in 1991 it was about $170 million – it had grown substantially already. In 1999 I came to New Zealand because I got a job offer at Auckland University. So I was a lecturer there. And then in 2001, two years later, the trade had grown to $1 billion. Exports to China had grown to $1 billion, about 3.3 per cent of total exports. And then last year when I became an MP exports to China had grown to almost $6 billion or 12 per cent of total exports.

This reflects the relationship between China and New Zealand. We are moving closer and my becoming an MP in New Zealand also highlights the change in society in New Zealand and the importance of the relationship. At the same time, of course, we see lots of opportunities but also challenges. Since I became an MP last November I've been to China twice. I'm leaving for China tonight – my third trip to China as an MP. As an MP, I can feel strongly the trust from the Chinese side – there is an extremely strong relationship between China and New Zealand. And that relationship is based on efforts over a long time – both Labour and National governments have been trying to foster the relationship.

We need to make sure the public really has a thorough, good, balanced view about China.

But in New Zealand of course we still have this domestic political issue. The New Zealand public still needs to know more about China. There is still misunderstanding about the growth of China and the rise of China. While in China that is not the issue at all about New Zealand. Chinese people do not have this particular concern about New Zealand. They all love New Zealand – a very positive perception. The only concern for the Chinese would be New Zealand in international relations. That is, when China has to deal with other great powers. The position of New Zealand – that is a concern for the Chinese government. It is not a domestic issue for the Chinese when it comes to New Zealand–China relations. So there is a very strong political relationship, very strong economic relationship. Very strong trust. And this trust can be, or could be, challenged when we are dealing with other great powers. So I believe the Prime Minister made a very good comment when he was saying that the growing influence of China in the South Pacific reflects its growing influence globally. That is a natural growth. So this kind of position I think is very well conceived. The Chinese tend to believe that New Zealand has a very constructive, balanced view about China.

So this is the challenge for the future. To reflect on the last 20 years, we can see the strong growth, we can see we are well-positioned for the future, but we can see the challenge. As I mentioned, domestic politics are very important, domestic opinion is very important. Fortunately we have very good institutions like the Asia New Zealand Foundation and now we have the new China Council, which I believe is extremely important because we need to make sure the public really has a thorough, good, balanced view about China. That will lay the foundations for our government's policies towards China.

—Dr Jian Yang

> What we need to focus on is not only trade. Trade is very important for us. And at this stage our vision for China is dominated by our economic relations. But at the same time we need strength in our social, cultural, political relations. The social relationship has been growing because we have more and more immigrants, for example. Culturally we have more cultural visitors, delegations visiting China. But we need to have a more comprehensive strategy to enhance our cultural exchanges with China which will, in the end, help the public to a better understanding of China. That will lay a foundation for a sustainable relationship.
>
> —*Dr Jian Yang*

What to do?

How do we convince the New Zealand public that we're on the right course? Many of you are aware that, about a millennium ago, there was a very interesting point of English history, the Battle of Hastings. Well, I was in our Hastings three months ago, and talking about things like Chinese investment, I got a barrage of pure xenophobia. And therefore, for me the New Zealand China Council has a real need to be able to respond to this sort of thing. If we go through another Crafar farm – I'll call it debacle – the New Zealand China Council will be on the speed dial of Morning Report and everything else. So I really want to know – what are the three or four things we have to do? Low-cost things that can be sustainable to help educate the people in Hastings, in Wairoa, in Greymouth, in Hokitika, in Gore, in Ashburton. It's not just Auckland or Wellington. We've got to take the whole country with us or we'll continue to have a lot of aggravation.

—*Sir Don McKinnon*

Lazy tabloid reporting

Despite the fact that a great deal of our economy and indeed our prosperity is tied to China, New Zealanders are woefully ignorant about China thanks to what can most charitably be described as an indifferent mainstream media. For the greater part, what coverage there is, is both ill-informed and tabloid and almost without exception looks for the sensational and the negative.

You need only listen to radio talk-back to get a sense of how ill-informed or uninformed the average New Zealander is about China. The Crafar farms is a perfect example of, in my view, appalling coverage. I don't have a problem with the debate about foreign ownership, but what I do have a problem about is the lack of broad discussion of this issue. A great deal flies under the radar and is not really touched upon by the fourth estate.

Examples that many of you will be aware of: the United States owns 35 per cent of our pine forests; well over 50 per cent of our much-famed wine industry is owned internationally; Shania Twain owns a good lump of the South Island high country; and there are significant Russian, Japanese and many other holdings in New Zealand, but not many people know that. It is not talked about.

So why then is the Crafar issue, and issues like that, given so much prominence? One could be forgiven for asking, is there a touch of xenophobia floating around? But I wouldn't ask that question, would I?

Companies must fall in love with China and genuinely embrace its richness, diversity and challenges.

In my view this lazy tabloid reporting has a very dark side and damages New Zealand. Audiences have no reliable context to assess China. They know little about China, Chinese history or culture or the larger benefits that accrue to NZ from Chinese investment, which is presented simply, as New Zealanders having something taken from them by China. It is for the large part an emotive position, not a factual one, and, in the information vacuum, it is a small step to suspicion and an "anti" position.

I have met NZ companies who have tried and failed in China. In all cases they assumed wrongly that it was the same as doing business anywhere else: they knew little or nothing about the importance of building relationships, they knew nothing

Prime Minister David Lange meets Rewi Alley at his home in Beijing, March 1986. (Photo: National Archives).

about Chinese culture, especially business culture, and nothing of our rich history with China. In short they were ill prepared; they expected to get on a plane with an order and to come home with it full!

This naivety must change if we are to engage at a level which is meaningful, enriching and productive for both countries. Companies must, in my view, fall in love with China and genuinely embrace its richness, diversity and challenges. They must become students in a world where everything has symbolism and where yes doesn't always mean yes, a world where negotiation is an art form. And metaphor is used in communicating ideas, for example, I was once asked why I thought documentaries were important: I described them as "bridges of understanding"

My advice is, homework and a lot of it. Avoid the expat enclave, move out of your comfort zone.

—Michael Stedman

Remarkable ignorance

The state of knowledge of each other in 1972 was very low. In China now the level of ignorance about New Zealand is utterly transformed. But the level of ignorance in New Zealand is still quite remarkable. The way to tackle this is through greater cooperation. For example, cooperation between museums, academics, in the area of film, is part of a necessary process. Chinese New Zealanders have a role to play in the efforts to change the poor state of knowledge. It's estimated that now one in every eight Aucklanders is Chinese. New Zealand has three Confucius Institutes. A key goal, especially in Auckland, is to facilitate schools introducing Chinese language into their curriculum. The past 40 years have seen a vast opening up of China to the outside, but perhaps less of an opening up of New Zealand to China.

—Prof. Paul Clark

More exchanges

People-to-people links – social, cultural, educational – are very important. Compared to economic links, they are often taken as natural outcomes, and not given a lot of attention. But people-to-people links are the foundation of bilateral relations, especially in a rapidly changing international environment. I'm glad to see an increase in Track 2 dialogues like this seminar. It's an area that needs policy support, and more effort from every circle – senior diplomats, professors. I look forward to more exchanges between think-tanks, universities, students at every level.

—Associate Professor Guo Chunmei

Discover China! martial arts class at Wellington High School. (Photo: Confucius Institute).

Cultural diplomacy

百闻不如一见

Seeing once is worth hearing about something 100 times

New Zealand's national museum, Te Papa Tongarewa, and cultural diplomacy in China

Cultural diplomacy, like "soft power", is one of those inexact international concepts that can defy a tight definition.

Professor Joseph Nye's depiction of "soft power" is the ability to get what you want through attraction rather than coercion or payment. So, "soft power" is influence that does not depend on economic power or military strength. Given New Zealand's comparative lack of "hard power" in global terms, soft power is very important to us, more obviously than it might be for larger countries.

A thoughtful explanation of cultural diplomacy has been provided by Professor Cynthia Schneider (Georgetown University) who has studied the impact of cultural influences in foreign policy. Herself a diplomat, Schneider sees cultural diplomacy as:

> an overall approach that involves much more than just sending our culture out there, that it involves, equally importantly, listening to and understanding cultures in other places and then using that understanding as a way to engage, build relationships, and ultimately achieve mutual goals. Today, cultural diplomacy is in a state of untapped potential.

So, cultural diplomacy, ultimately, is about the voice of a people, speaking to another; the ear of a people, listening to the other; and the eye of a people, appreciating the other. For the long term. . . .

It should follow, therefore, that integrating cultural diplomacy into foreign policy-making makes good sense. As New Zealand and China become increasingly connected bilaterally and through regional security policies, trade flows and people-to-people links, a closeness in cultural affinity and attitudes becomes ever more important. A relationship that is merely transactional "builds no belonging, loyalty or community", as the Australian commentator, Michael Wesley, has said. We need a relationship "in the round", as Chris Elder has mentioned. Indeed, our future depends on it.

It too follows that the role of museums in cultural diplomacy is an important one. Museums connect diverse communities and their shared and complex heritage. Museums do this within a country, with partners such as the Confucius Institutes, schools and universities and community groups, and with partners around the world.

The global "reach" of museums and exhibitions can not only enhance the international reputation of their nations but also have a direct human impact. The shared human response to beauty, art and creative experience can bridge those differences in language, traditions and history, which, despite "globalisation", still hinder cross-cultural communication and understanding.

A striking example of the power of culture to transcend place and time is a painting by Rita Angus, one of New Zealand's most important artists and much loved (see p.80). It is one of three famous "goddess" paintings by Angus, celebrating her view that women possess a mystical power to bring peace.

Note the hands of this "goddess" and the flower, the willow branches over her head, and the pattern of Chinese ceramics of her skirt.

The biographer of Rita Angus, Jill Trevelyan, has noted that Angus would have seen an incredible exhibition of Chinese art that toured New Zealand in 1937, which included a bronze Guanyin.

This extraordinary show of over 400 ancient bronzes, jade (including cong 琮 and bi 璧), Han and Tang figurines, celadon and porcelain, had a profound influence on the New Zealand public.

In a direct and practical way, most New Zealanders saw, and responded to a China that, hitherto, they had only thought of as backward and poverty-stricken. Now, they were looking at the material culture of one of the longest and richest civilizations in the history of the world. For many, including artists and scholars, the exhibition was a revelation.

Mainstream New Zealand society in 1937 was predominantly European. There must also have been Māori and local Chinese visitors to the exhibition but we don't so far have accounts of their responses. Unlike today, New Zealand's Chinese community in the 1930s/40s was not large. Some would have been descended from the first migrants to New Zealand in the 1860s.

With what emotion, I wonder – pride? longing? indifference? – did they view those objects, which had begun to symbolise the idea of "China" in the minds of their New Zealand compatriots? Did a shared response to beauty and art bring the two groups together, however briefly? I would like to think so.

Yet another important impact of the exhibition was the realisation that Māori and Chinese cultures share similarities. For example, there are very few jade cultures in the world. You and we have two of them. In his introduction to the exhibition, Dr Perceval Yetts (Professor of Chinese Art and Archaeology, University of London) wrote:

> For New Zealanders, Chinese art may be said to offer a special interest, because of certain similarities with Māori ornament. Here is a promising field of research, which might reveal fresh clues to the great enigmas of both Māori and Chinese origins.

Since 1937, the flow of cultural exchange between our two countries, has comprised art, music, dance, literature, film, documentaries, sport – and even

Rita Angus, *A Goddess of Mercy*, 1945–47. Collection of Christchurch Art Gallery Te Puna o Waiwhetu. Reproduced courtesy of the Estate of Rita Angus.

gardens. New Zealand presented a unique pavilion – with a roof garden – at the Shanghai World Expo, and we were proud participants in the Beijing Olympics. But the 1937 experience remains an early example of cultural diplomacy in that it profoundly changed the perceptions of China in the minds of a people who were about as far flung from here as you could imagine, not only in terms of physical distance but also in thought, tradition and history.

This year the national museum of New Zealand, Te Papa, has been delighted to celebrate the 40th anniversary with not one, but three significant exhibitions, which opened in China in October.

In offering Chinese audiences a direct experience of New Zealand culture, in their own country, Te Papa is helping to connect two peoples, just as, within Aotearoa New Zealand, Te Papa is a public sphere that attracts many communities, both domestic and external. People come to Te Papa – and come together in Te Papa – to be inspired, stimulated, and understood.

Te Papa is privileged to have as our major Chinese partner, the National Museum of China. It is one of the world's largest museums, with state-of-the-art facilities. We enjoy a close partnership with this great museum and a shared commitment to ongoing exchanges.

Te Papa also has excellent relationships with other major museums, among them the China Art Museum in Shanghai, the Shaanxi History Museum in Xian (surely one of the world's greatest treasure houses) and the China Three Gorges Museum in Chongqing. In addition to Beijing and Shanghai, we are planning to bring Aotearoa New Zealand's treasures to Hangzhou, Guangzhou, Chongqing and Xian over the next 18 months. In sharing our cultural heritage with Chinese audiences nationwide, we are privileged at the same time to be gaining insight into China's heritage.

These flagship museums reflect the liveliness of cultural activity in China. There is a perceptible buzz around museums, with new ones being built and old ones renewed. This year, every museum that I have visited has been filled with students, children and adults alike. They seem to enjoy being surrounded by the vast and varied treasures of China's past, as well as contemporary times.

This enthusiasm, encouraged by the Chinese Government (which is highly engaged in cultural diplomacy, for example with the 400 Confucius Institutes in over 100 countries), makes it a particularly exciting time for New Zealand and others to be connecting with China around art and culture and to be thinking about issues such as the transformational role of art and culture in contemporary Chinese society and politics.

Just as China at the geopolitical level is reflecting on its place in the world, what reflections are there of Chinese culture in the 21st century? In what ways would Chinese culture continue to influence the world as it has for millennia? We in Te Papa would welcome the chance to explore such issues.

—Wen Powles

Cultural diplomacy: countertenor Xiao Ma performing in Wellington. (Photo: Confucius Institute).

Professor Manying Ip speaks of her experiences as a Chinese New Zealander.

New Zealand's Chinese community

入乡随俗

When you enter a country, attend to its customs

A new home

The number of Chinese moving permanently to New Zealand is growing. China is New Zealand's second largest source of migrants after the United Kingdom. Over 26,000 Chinese decided to make New Zealand a new home during the last four years. That number is more than the size of New Zealand's entire ethnic Chinese community just a generation ago. The next census will likely show a resident population of Chinese in New Zealand of close to 200,0000 people – ten times bigger than a generation ago.

—*Carl Worker*

Recognising Diversity

On this topic on diversity, I want to talk about the New Zealand watershed years since 1987. I would suggest that diversity offers a good chance to everyone. And there's the PC way of saying that diversity needs to be embraced and celebrated. But I think that diversity needs to be recognised before it is embraced and celebrated. So I will try to share some basic information about what the scene is like. And also, why diversity is challenging, particularly in New Zealand, and what the effect is of conflating "Chinese" and "Asians" in general in New Zealand.

I arrived in the country in the early 70s, and as you know, in the 1970s New Zealand was supposedly a race relations haven. It was only in the 1980s, after I finished my Ph.D., that by chance I discovered the (Chinese) poll tax boxes and re-entry permits in the National archives. That was the first time I knew that we had had an unwritten white New Zealand policy. I found the poll tax certificates and the requirement for Chinese to pay £100 to enter New Zealand. And the re-entry permit that any Chinese leaving the country would have to apply for – every ethnic Chinese needed to have a re-entry permit to leave and re-enter New Zealand. It was very clearly illustrated in our national archives that when we talk about immigrants, "immigrant" somehow was conflated with "Chinese". Even local-born Chinese were counted as immigrants. This is really against nationality law and international law.

This existed in New Zealand and that is why we need to talk about how long an immigrant must stay in the country before that person is considered a citizen. Increasingly in contemporary times, New Zealand citizens are being replaced by non-citizens, and many of the latter are Asian. Of course, that means increasing ethnic diversity for New Zealand. Asians are not the only immigrant group, but

NZ Population Born in Northeast Asia 2006

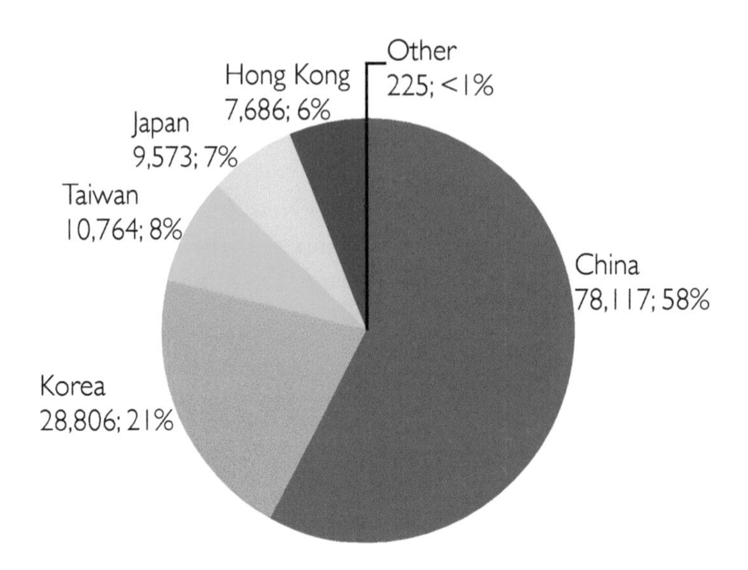

Birthplaces of the Usually Resident Population Who Identify as Chinese; New Zealand 2006

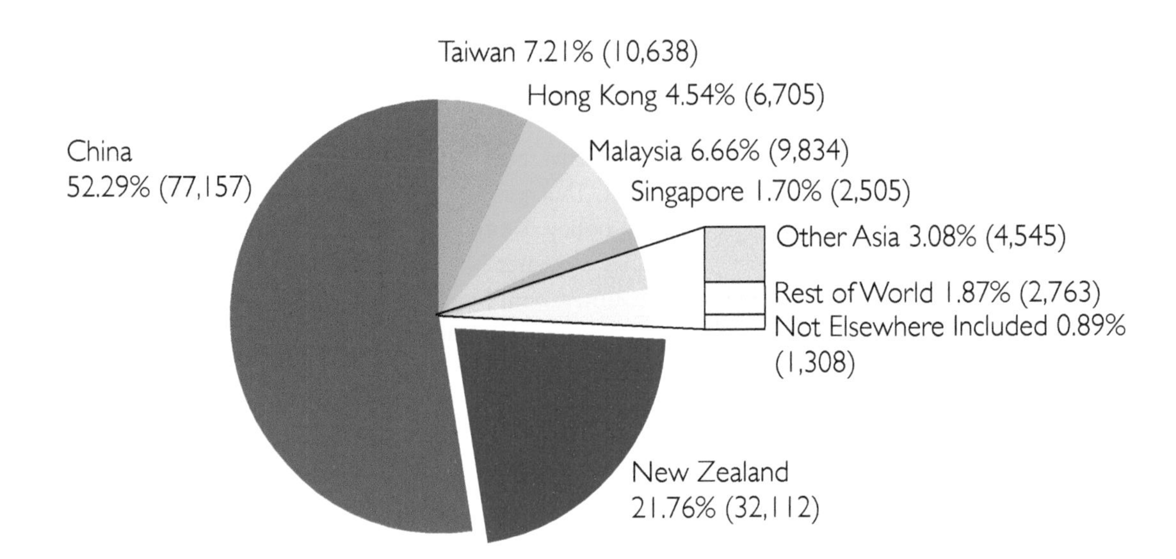

Statistics NZ 2006 Census

they are the most visible group. The Chinese are always a visible minority. If you have German immigrants, for argument's sake, as long as he or she keeps their mouth shut, then no one would know that they are from Germany

Cultural diversity is a fact now, and it will not go back. We cannot just go to sleep and hope that it will change. It won't. It will only change to be browner and yellower and a deeper colour. I mean New Zealand itself will be a deeper colour. As a pragmatic illustration, talking about health services, according to an article in the New Zealand Medical Journal, 34 per cent of the population served by the Auckland District Health Board will be Asian by 2016. So Asians are present everywhere, and many of them are Chinese.

The ultimate challenge is how to build an inclusive New Zealand identity

Actually, in New Zealand popular parlance, we talk about Asians as if they were all Chinese or East Asians, but according to Statistics New Zealand there is a division into East Asian, Southeast Asian, and South Asian. Those who are of Chinese ethnicity are from China and Taiwan, and they belong to the East Asian group. Within Asia, Northeast Asia is the largest contributor, in terms of immigrants entering the country. Among the Northeast Asians, we have people from China, from Hong Kong, from Taiwan, and we count Japan and Korea in Northeast Asia as well. Of the ethnic Chinese population, in 2006 21 per cent were actually born in New Zealand – born and bred here. And then, a much smaller percentage – 7 per cent – Taiwan born. And only 4.5 per cent Hong Kong born.

Policy-makers are dealing with people who have really quite different subcultures, different languages and different dialects. These groups have different political experience, and different levels of political participation. Some come from a Socialist background – the PRC – and some are used to working within an electoral system, like the Taiwanese, or there are the Hong Kong people who are much more apolitical. But the perception is that we are all just part of "China".

Why is diversity challenging? Well, I would suggest that Chineseness has long been juxtaposed as the opposite to New Zealandness or Kiwiness, whatever the latter is. In the past, in the goldmining days, New Zealand culture was supposed to be Christian, and a typical New Zealander was the hard-working, honest bloke. At that time Chineseness was portrayed as opium-smoking, gambling, and all sorts of dishonesty. That was so-called Chineseness in the 19th century. Right now, of course, Chineseness is different. Chineseness is having lots of money, buying up Africa, buying up the South Pacific, or in the community it's driving BMWs and Mercedes. Whereas New Zealanders are much more low-key and humble and so on. Whatever Chineseness is, it is for the most part somehow opposite to what Kiwiness is.

It is pretty hard for immigrants to try to fit the so-called Kiwi culture, because Kiwi culture, New Zealand culture, changes. How would you characterise New Zealand culture? It changes from the 19th to the 20th century, and again in the 21st century. So now it takes on the "can-do" attitude, and probably it's not so much against tall poppies. It is continually changing and it is quite hard for Chineseness to catch up. Moreoever, national identity is assumed to be static, and then it doesn't seem that Chineseness is contributing to it.

A wariness towards immigrants is very understandable and [Frankland slide 13] so is a concern that the population may be "genetically modified" by the changing proportion of different ethnic groups within the whole.

If you look at trends over the past two or three censuses, you can see that Mandarin and Cantonese are becoming increasingly more important languages in New Zealand, just as China is rising in the list of birthplaces of overseas-born New Zealand residents. Analysis of demographic characteristics, education levels, and language ability all point to the potential to make use of this immigrant base to contribute to a closer relationship between New Zealand and Asia. They are well educated, they are young, they have multiple language indicators. They are people who have real experience in China and all around Asia, and have experience in and goodwill towards New Zealand.

At the moment, many of the new migrants adopt a transnational lifestyle. This should not be regarded as a sign of unsuccessful integration. Popular opinion regards people moving around as being disloyal to New Zealand or as unsuccessful immigrants. But we should stop thinking like that and consider also the relocation of the second generation, which could be regarded as an enrichment of social and cultural capital for New Zealand. Different generations in fact have different trajectories so you could have the parents here, the grandparents in China, and then the young ones moving all around, or else the other way round. These transmigrants are never really uprooted and they would not need transplanting because they are a different kind of plant. When looking at transmigrants, we need to shift our thinking around.

We are witnessing now the incessant trajectory of people between New Zealand, Australia, and China. We may call them settlers in New Zealand or we call them back-door migrants to Australia, or returnees to the China region. Some destinations will feature more prominently than others at different times, depending on the economic climate, depending on how well things are going generally. But this will be the trajectory that we will experience in the next 10 to 15 years. And we could make good use of the people who are moving around like that.

Within the Chinese ethnicity, there is diversity. "Chinese" is a very heterogeneous group, and so are the Chinese communities in New Zealand. Moreover, they differ in the history of their settlement. We have got fifth-generation New Zealanders. We have got more recent migrants, who are from the 1980s, 1990s onwards, and they are different in their socio-economic status, in their English ability, and in their acculturation. But they have made a very strong imprint on New Zealand social development, and in politics, economics, and also the arts.

The ultimate challenge is how to build an inclusive New Zealand identity. By inclusive I mean, for example, if Manying Ip walks down Queen Street, people would not ask me to go home. That is, as Jian Yang was saying, one day it would be socially acceptable to be a Chinese New Zealander. And if I want to talk to Māori people discussing the Treaty, "I think that – this and that", and not have people looking sideways at me. "You, talking about the Treaty? It's a New Zealand thing. Not for you, you know". To have an inclusive kind of identity given to the Chinese as well as others would of course be much better for the Chinese New Zealanders. But more importantly, it would be much better for New Zealand.

—Manying Ip

The main point in my talk was, when would immigrants be regarded as true New Zealanders? The Chinese faced legislative discrimination in the old days. But now we face an invisible kind of social kind of "othering". Jian Yang talked about the kind of trust which has not yet been accorded to all New Zealanders. This is a general issue of national identity, that is, what New Zealand wants to become. Personally I believe that the Chinese and other Asians and all immigrants would have a big part to play because everyone is contributing to this New Zealand identity, so let's all engage in a real, ongoing, intelligent conversation about what New Zealand identity is, and what being a New Zealander is about.
—Manying Ip

Feeling like I belong

First of all, let me answer why I am here. Why New Zealand, why not some other country that I could go to study? My parents asked my brother and me – about 10 years ago, my brother was 14, I was 18 – if you had an opportunity to go overseas to study, would you like to? Both of us were very excited and we decided that's what we wanted to do. It was New Zealand because my cousin's family had already moved here, so my parents knew that if they sent two young children to New Zealand, somebody would look after us. Another thing, New Zealand back then was cheaper than the US and the UK. I clearly remember three Chinese yuan were equal to one New Zealand dollar – after three years that changed. And also the most important reason was because it still had a reputation for being a safe and green and friendly country for international students. And so we came in 2003.

To summarise, I want to talk about the three stages of my life in New Zealand so far, and the challenges I came across during those stages and how I overcame them. The biggest challenge was that the first few months after I arrived were completely different from what I had imagined. Because I lived with my cousin's family we would speak Chinese every day, watch Chinese soap opera online, and read Chinese newspapers. I called my mum and told her look, apart from the sky is very blue, the grass is very green, what's the big difference? I still felt like I was living in China except I was extremely homesick. So my mum and my dad told me that, be patient, things will change. It's a new country and what you need to do first is to learn the language and you will be able to get out there and make friends. And that's exactly what I did.

If you know what you want to get out of your experience, and you trust yourself and never steer away too far from what you really believe, most of the time things turn out to be all right.

So things got better when I enrolled at university but the second challenge came, which is the drinking culture. I couldn't drink. And all my university friends, especially local Kiwi students, they loved drinking, and I found it very hard to fit in. Also, I had a strong sense that local students were not really interested in me. I don't know about other students, but I didn't really feel like they wanted to know where I was from. And because my English wasn't that good back then, at uni they had a lot of group discussions. I really didn't like it, because they didn't have time to wait for me to come across with the right words to express myself. They had already moved on to the next topic. I felt I was left behind and there were times when I had doubts about my intelligence. I thought maybe I was just slow. But as my language got better and better I realized, brilliant, finally I can have an argument and have a debate to get my point across. And that's the moment when I found that the most valuable thing I learnt from university is to get my English to a point that I can make myself heard.

The drinking part of it I failed, but how I made friends was through sports. I love soccer, I played squash, I joined the Auckland canoeing club, we went white-water rafting, and through all these outdoor activities I made friends with people from all around the world. Even today, some of these people are still my closest friends. I'll give you an example: the Olympic Games opening night – opening morning in New Zealand. I watched it with six of my closest friends, and they're from Germany, the United States, Japan, Argentina and my partner's a Norwegian. And also my closest friend, she's from Malaysia. So it's quite interesting when each of our countries' team walks out. We all make fun of each other, judging their outfits. But when the New Zealand team walked out, we all stood up and we cheered. It was great to see the New Zealand flag come out and that's something we all shared in common. This is the country we had all lived in for five years – for more than five years for most of these people. And this is what we call our second home, and that's something we celebrated in common.

So move on to the third challenge, which was when I started working. My very first job was at a big magazine publishing company. My job was advertising accounts administration. My main job was to check that all the advertisements put into the magazine were in the right place, and that we charged the client the right amount of money. So actually, it was more accounts-related than anything to do with culture or editorial stuff. I realised most of the stories were tabloid or about relationships. There was nothing relevant to me. The only two things I got involved with relating to my culture were two stories. One was the Little Pumpkin story – I'm not sure if you remember that. They came to my Korean manager and asked if she could speak Chinese. And my Korean manager said no, I'm Korean, but my colleague here, Liyang, she can speak Chinese. And that's when the magazine editor got in touch with me and asked me to do some translations and do the initial interview with Little Pumpkin's family back in China. And the second story I was involved with was Miss Huang Chen, which was a very unfortunate story. She was robbed in South Auckland and the people decided to run over her in a car. And so I interviewed her father and the family. So that was the second story coming through the magazine. And these are not the positive side of what my community can offer.

So I have to say, that first job experience wasn't the most satisfying. But I learnt a lot of things from there. And I think because of that, I started looking for things interesting to do that I found relevant to me. So I volunteered at Auckland Lantern Festival, and two years after volunteering at the festival I met my current employer Asia New Zealand Foundation, and two years later I got a job at the Wellington office working on the culture programme. And after a while I moved back to Auckland, based in our Auckland office. I have to say I feel very fortunate to be part of the team that is helping New Zealanders to understand more about Asia. In April my manager, Jennifer King, and I travelled to China together. That was a very special trip for me. I go home every year to visit my family, but it was the first time I had gone home from a different perspective. The purpose of the trip was to meet with lantern makers who provide lanterns for the lantern festival. We also met people from the Ministry of Culture in China, who helped us by sending the international performers from China to New Zealand. Jennifer and I and my team of colleagues would host these international performers. And also we met some arts organisations where we could do artistic exchanges, attracting Chinese artists coming to New Zealand and also sending New Zealand artists to China. I think through culture and arts is a great way to tell a story and make people understand each other.

It took me six years to finally say that I felt like I belonged. How I knew I did was because one of my colleagues said she was going to the UK to work and that's her big OE. And I said, "I wish I had that opportunity". And she said, "What are you talking about? You've been doing your OE for the past eight years". And that clicked. I realised I'm so used to being here I forgot I'm in New Zealand.

Another thing that really helped me go through a lot of challenges is to keep in regular contact with my family and with my friends at home. They are the people that keep me grounded. They keep reminding me why I'm here, and when things get hard they remind me of the values and the principles, and I think the Prime Minister mentioned openness, honesty, and those apply to what I've been brought up with. So I think if you know what you want to get out of your experience, and you trust yourself and never steer away too far from what you really believe, most of the time things turn out to be all right.

—*Liyang Ma*

PART 4

NEW ZEALAND AND CHINA IN THE ASIA-PACIFIC REGION

The regional context

风雨同舟

In the same boat in the wind and the rain

Shaping institutions

When we talk about New Zealand and China in the region, we need to consider also how our bilateral relations bear on regional issues and see the bilateral relations in a regional context. When we talk in a regional context, New Zealand often disappears into a large group of countries, and China into consideration of China–United States relations. How can our two countries relate on regional issues?

The area involved is large, and the attempts at regional institutions in the past have had to accommodate big membership numbers, often in a region-wide fashion. It is interesting to note, however, that, in recent years, the Trans-Pacific Partnership (TPP) started with four small countries and has expanded to 11 now. The Regional Comprehensive Economic Partnership (RCEP) has a membership of 16, which is still manageable. With these two, the evolution of regional institutions comes to a critical conjecture. Viewed from a geopolitical point of view, the security situation that shaped up in the region in the past several years also sees such subtle or soft subregional groupings around a set of different issues – territorial issues, big-country interests, alliances, etc.

How should we regard the region as a whole? For China, the divisions are perhaps rather more clear. In the region it sees Northeast Asian neighbouring countries first and foremost, Southeast Asia, New Zealand and Australia, Pacific Islands, with varied levels of importance to China. We need to consider what common interests and opportunities we see in these areas. For regional institutions, for example, China is involved with the RCEP, and the United States is part of TPP. New Zealand is a member of both. There is scope to work together in a regional context. New Zealand has both the capacity and the competency to make a useful input. NZ–China relations therefore will be very relevant to the shaping of regional institutions and regional order.

—*Prof. Xiaoming Huang*

Strategic cooperation

In China's eyes, the Asia-Pacific region is very confused, and presents many challenges. If we look at the challenges in a positive way we can address the problems that exist. The way forward is to enhance economic cooperation and based on this build up trust and develop political cooperation. The biggest change recently has been the negative impact of the global economic crisis.

How can we transform "strategic competition" on a political level to strategic cooperation? New Zealand is the most independent of all the developed countries. Its diplomatic posture is not much influenced by the views of other developed countries. I'm positive about the future of relations between us. We share common values. For instance, the US and the EU want to discuss human values only from their own perspective. It's better to do so from the perspective of the interests of the people involved.

—*Shi Yongming*

Follow the money

The possibilities for cooperation in strategic areas have grown over time. This is true of both bilateral and multilateral cooperation.

The Asia-Pacific region is characterised by "anarchic regimes", whose mode of decision-making is to work through compromise and consensus. Mutual interests come together for mutual benefit. North America said that this approach would not deliver results, but they were wrong in this. A great deal has been accomplished. For instance, at the time of the 1999 APEC meeting in Auckland, a breakout meeting on East Timor led to the creation of a humanitarian mission.

The United States rebalancing is seeing the redeployment of the US navy in the Pacific, and improved security cooperation with its partners in the region. The United States now plays a bigger role in Asia-Pacific security thinking.

Are we witnessing a zero-sum game? Is the US rebalancing a direct response to Chinese expansion? I don't believe that is necessarily the case. It is explicable rather in terms of the United States desire to "follow the money". The Asia-Pacific region is now the lynchpin of the global economic system.

The number of actors who need to be accommodated is starting to grow

New Zealand has been affected by the rebalancing. Its strategic relationship with the United States has warmed considerably. That has been manifested in high-level visits, the Wellington and Washington declarations, the return of joint military training, and the possibility of cooperation in other areas in the future.

There should not be concern that New Zealand is getting caught up in a zero-sum game – a straight balance-of-power struggle between the United States and China. Rather, the number of actors who need to be accommodated is starting to grow.

The South Pacific is of importance economically and politically. China is beginning to play a bigger role there. This offers New Zealand and Australia the possibility of cooperating rather than competing with China. The recently announced trilateral water project in the Cook Islands is an example of what may be achieved.

China is hardly alone in showing an enhanced interest in the South Pacific. Japan, Korea, the countries of Southeast Asia, India, and Russia are among the countries becoming more involved. The South Pacific has now become very crowded.

What is evident is a "soft balancing" – not a traditional balance-of-power approach, but balance-of-power behaviour within institutions. Strategic competition is not inevitable. Doors are being opened to greater consultation and cooperation. The Pacific is very big. There is room for everyone.

—*Marc Lanteigne*

Structural change

Economic relations in the Asia-Pacific region have gone through three stages. The first was from 1960 to 1980 when the region went through a process of catching up and market integration, led by the United States. It was marked by Japan's economic recovery, and the emergence of the "four dragons" – the East Asian "economic miracle". Over the period, there was a significant increase in the business conducted between the United States and East Asia.

The second was from the 1980s through to 2008. Over that time the role of the United States changed from that of an import market to that of a participant in intra-regional trade. The third stage, from 2008 on, is seeing structural change in response to the sub-prime credit crisis. There is a lot of pressure to restructure the paradigm of supply and demand. In East Asia there is a need to change from export-led growth to internal consumption and a sustained growth model.

The United States first of all tried to rebuild the Asia-Pacific economic institutions based on APEC. Then it moved to bilateral and plurilateral FTAs. Its aim has been to open up the East Asian market and regain competitiveness. We are at a point where the United States itself has to change, rather than just put pressure on others to change.

China and New Zealand have common interests in the Asia-Pacific region. We are both members of APEC, we both have our major market share in the Asia-Pacific. The free trade agreement between us is a model agreement. The Trans-Pacific Partnership excludes China, but the Regional Comprehensive Economic Partnership provides a framework the two countries can cooperate within. New Zealand could play a role in bridging the gap between the TPP and the RCEP.

The Chinese economy is in the process of restructuring and rebalancing. China is interested in promoting a free trade area involving China, Japan and Korea, and in the RCEP. It has no current role in the TPP.

We are at a point where the United States itself has to change, rather than just put pressure on others to change.

In the future, the Chinese economy will play a larger role in East Asia and the Asia-Pacific region as a growth engine, leading demand through its large domestic market, and the main source of FDI. I'm confident that China will take a more active role in regional trade groups, and keep an open mind on the TPP. I hope we can find a approach that will enable us to cooperate in working towards regional economic integration.

—*Prof. Zhang Yunling*

Regional strategies and concerns

China's foreign strategy takes big power relations as the key; the neighbouring area as the priority; the developing world as the foundation; and a multiple approach as the platform. All these elements can easily be found in East Asia. In other words, China's regional strategy very much overlaps with its global strategy.

China's regional interests lie in stability; maintaining a peaceful international environment to permit domestic modernisation; friendship; recognition of the importance of regional power relations and regional systems; cooperation; integrating Chinese interests with the region; entering into partnerships; and fostering a common regional sense and identity. In short, what China is trying to do is to respect regional differences, to dilute regional contradictions, and to go beyond the geopolitical barrier.

Chinese security concerns centre on achieving domestic stability, unity and territorial integrity; social prosperity through consistent economic and social reform and development in a Chinese way; peace and stability in Asia; and as a matter of principle shelving disputes and pursuing joint development. Examples are the Declaration on the Conduct of Parties in South China Sea (DOC), the Code of Conduct (COC) derived from the Guidelines on the Implementation of the DOC, the Southeast Asia Nuclear Free Zone, China's Defence White Paper, the Treaty of Amity and Cooperation, and so on.

The New Zealand regional strategy, in the light of New Zealand government pronouncements, can be seen as the following:

- The New Zealand Government supports regional integration in Asia as a means to economic transformation and the growth of the Asian economies;

- The government will sustain its strong commitment to leadership diplomacy and top level engagement with Asia;
- The government will ensure that enough attention is paid to China and India;
- New Zealand will deepen its relationship with ASEAN and with its key members, both through regional processes and through bilateral connections.

The shift of economic influence to Asia over recent years has Japan, China and the Republic of Korea at its centre. These three North Asian countries are increasingly important for New Zealand as economic and trading partners, and their weight in international political and regional strategic affairs is increasing. China in particular is growing rapidly in importance both bilaterally and regionally.

Sino-New Zealand perceptions of the region are strongly focused on regional integration as a direction, and on stability as a process, while China is more concerned about the internal reform process and social adaptability, and New Zealand is more concerned about changes in the regional economic structure, to a large extent based on the Chinese economy. Therefore, China's requirement in the region can be simply interpreted as guarantees for, and promotion of, domestic reform. China's evolving participation in the regional and international community is still strongly dependent on the success of internal economic and social reform.

—Prof. Han Feng

Coordinating relations

I will make three points. One is in terms of bilateral relations. In addition to the good feeling of the Chinese public towards New Zealand, I think New Zealand's national characteristics are also helpful. As a developed country New Zealand's location is far away from the developed camp centralised in Europe and North America. New Zealand is without any negative record in history. So it's more acceptable to the Chinese public as a western country.

Two: in China's understanding, economic development and regional integration may gradually penetrate to the social development level. Eventually it may penetrate to the political field as well, to promote a smooth and more gradual Chinese involvement in the region or in the so-called international community. This has been put forward by Deng Xiaoping, but it is also an East Asian regional experience, especially with the integration process of Southeast Asia, or ASEAN.

The last point is it seems to me that so-called globalisation is going against power relations to some extent. For example the emergence of China is partly because of Chinese efforts domestically. But it is also a result of the industrial readjustment or changes at the regional level or the global level. You can see in this area we have raised industrial development dramatically, from Japan and the four tigers and then China. Maybe we can see India, Indonesia, Vietnam in the following-on position. So this is the consequence of globalisation rather than purely a Chinese design or arrangement.

But you know, in terms of power relations, the picture is quite different. So how can we balance this? Also we saw formal relations between the United States and Japan in this area. So we try to coordinate relations at the regional level as well as the global level. Another point is that the regional system arrangement is a kind of regional domain, I think dominated by ASEAN as a whole. So we can see the regional arrangement without the United States as a first point, and ASEAN+ as a second. The most important ones are the ASEAN+1, +3, +6, +8. So this is a picture the United States is not going to see in terms of [favouring] the United States regional interests and power relations.

—*Prof. Han Feng*

Professor Han Feng (right) in conversation with Professor Xiaoming Huang, Director of the New Zealand Contemporary China Research Centre.

The South Pacific

众擎易举

Many hands make the lifting easy

A trilateral partnership in the Pacific

Over the last three years the government has redirected the focus of our international development assistance into the Pacific region where China is an increasingly important power. And as you heard the Prime Minister announce this morning, last week in the Cook Islands for the first time there was a trilateral partnership announced with the lead of the Cook Islands, and New Zealand and China as the partners. It seems to us, of course, in the international development group, a very positive development . . . it is, as Vice Minister Sui mentioned last week, a world first – another world first – for China and New Zealand.

—*Amanda Ellis*

Bringing players together

I think it's an extraordinarily good thing that China and New Zealand are working together on the water resource programme that's been mentioned this morning. In my recent experience in my work in Indonesia, in Kazakhstan, in Cambodia, and elsewhere, Chinese aid – and trade – but Chinese aid in particular, tends to be somewhat segregated, as does American aid. And so steps to bring together players in this field are extraordinarily positive. And particularly since Chinese aid is now such a vital component of the aid world in Africa, and in the South Pacific, as well as in many parts of East and Southeast Asia. We don't want a state of affairs in which the Cambodian Prime Minister, Mr Hun Sen, can say – as he has done more than once – I love Chinese aid because it comes on its own, without conditions, and is so much easier to manage than aid from other donors. We want the situation in which he will say, I'm delighted that Chinese aid is being given in conjunction with aid from New Zealand or other donors.

—*Peter Harris*

Mutual trust

May I make some comment here, as an outsider, and as an insider. Some of you may know I published a book in November last year, entitled *China in the South Pacific – Small States, Big Gains*. In the book I've suggested that we can understand the Chinese strategy in the South Pacific, and we should appreciate Chinese policy. But at the same time I agree that China should cooperate with other countries in terms of aid.

Now, as an insider, last March I was in China with Hon. Tim Groser. We talked about this project with Chinese leaders. At that time I personally believed that it was a great idea for the Chinese to cooperate with New Zealanders because we have such strong trust between us. And it will also project the Chinese image in the South Pacific in a more positive way. I believe this cooperation is based on mutual trust, and without strong mutual trust I don't think this would happen. So this case highlights the solid foundation for cooperation between China and New Zealand.

I believe that in the future New Zealand and China can do more in the region. I also want to emphasise that China in the South Pacific cannot be perceived as a threat. We should appreciate Chinese help. But of course we should try to make sure that Chinese aid to the region can be more productive, and more helpful and beneficial, to the local people in the region.

—Dr Jian Yang

More comprehensive relations

China has established a special forum for dealing with relations with the South Pacific in general. That was done by Premier Wen Jiabao in 2006. I think the main purpose is to coordinate the Chinese relations from the business-oriented to more comprehensive relations – political to economic, to investment, to regional development. You can see that some achievements have been made in this area. It has dramatically stopped the political competition between Taiwan and Mainland China.

—Prof. Han Feng

The fifth first

I welcome that – the "fifth first". It really does make sense that we have coordination. We do coordination with small countries in the Pacific, with Australia, with the European Union, with the Americans. China's now a big player in this area. It's really important that little countries don't have 20 different countries coming at them with conflicting aid programmes and objectives. And if we can do away with competition in the way that has happened in the past between Taiwan and the People's Republic of China, everybody will be better off.

—Phil Goff

PART 5
THE NEXT FORTY YEARS

China rising

事在人为

Success depends on the actions of man

Forecast and International Comparison of the Chinese Economy to 2025

I. Introduction

Since reform and opening up, the Chinese economy has experienced about 10 per cent average annual growth rate. However, after the global financial crisis, with the low growth rate of overseas developed-economies and the gradual shrinking of the new domestic workforce, as well as the constraints of domestic resources and environment, what lies ahead for China's potential economic growth? Can the astounding success in the past 30 years guarantee steady and rapid growth in the future? These are the problems attracting public attention.

A wealth of literature has focused on the medium- and long-term forecast for the Chinese economy, including the forecasts before 2009 and the ones after the start of the global financial crisis. However, the forecasts made by different researchers and institutions differ greatly, and no consensus has been reached on the medium- and long-term potential growth rate of the Chinese economy.

With major factors affecting the future economic growth of China taken into account, we further studied the medium- and long-term potential growth rate of the Chinese economy to 2025 based on new data and compared it to some developed economies.

II. Main factors influencing China's potential growth to 2025

(1) Population and labour force growth rates

The size and structure of the population are significant indicators reflecting the economic development, resource allocation, social security and so on of a country or region. China's population has increased to 1.346 billion in 2011 from 0.987 billion in 1980, with the growth rate falling from 1.67 per cent in 1987 to 0.48 per cent in 2010. Based on the statistical data on the fertility rate, death rate by age, gender ratio at birth and so on, it is estimated that the annual growth rates of China's population and labour force will decrease during 2011–2025.

(2) Urbanisation rate: the ratio of urban population to total population
On the one hand, the urbanisation rate directly affects investment in fixed assets as a higher urbanisation rate means more investment in roads, transportation facilities, real estate and so on. So urbanisation affects the investment as well as capital information and capital stock first, and then affects the potential economic growth in the medium- and long-term. On the other hand, the process of urbanisation means overall labour productivity and TFP will be raised with a higher urbanisation rate as more of the rural population will transfer to cities and towns to participate in the secondary and tertiary industries, which are more productive than primary industry.

Urbanisation rate
Since reform and opening up, the urbanisation rate has increased to 47.5 per cent in 2010 from 17.9 per cent in 1978, increasing by 29.6 percentage points and with average annual rise of 0.92 percentage points. Meanwhile about 200 or 300 million of the rural population transferred to cities and towns. The urbanisation rate will continue to increase during 2011–2025.

(3) R&D inputs
The R&D inputs are effective in improving TFP according to economics. The ratio of R&D inputs to GDP was 1.8 per cent in 2010, and it is estimated to be 2.01 per cent, 2.23 per cent and 2.42 per cent respectively in 2015, 2020 and 2025 under the baseline scenario, maintaining the increasing trend.

(4) The ratio of fiscal expenditure on education to GDP
Education is effective in increasing labour quality and human capital. The ratio of fiscal expenditure on education to GDP first reduced, then increased since reform and opening up, with the ratio decreasing from 5.1 per cent in 1980 to 2.3 per cent in 1995, decreasing by 0.18 per cent annually; but it has increased to 3.57 per cent in 2010, growing by 0.08 percentage points annually, due to more support for education from the government. The ratio of fiscal expenditure on education to GDP will increase gradually during 2011–2025.

(5) Global economic environment
On the one hand, the changes in the global economy first influence exports; then investment in manufacturing as well as capital formation and capital stock; and finally will affect the potential economic growth in the medium- and long-term. On the other hand, the host country's TFP will be raised thanks to FDI's positive spillover effect in management and technology, and more FDI increases this positive effect. The growth rates of both the global economy and FDI to China are likely to decrease during 2011–2025.

III. Scenario designs and forecasts of China's economy to 2025

Three scenarios have been designed covering 2011–2025: baseline, optimistic and pessimistic scenarios, including five exogenous variables: population growth rate, urbanisation rate, ratio of fiscal expenditure on education to GDP, ratio of R&D expenditure to GDP, and growth rate of the world GDP.

Design of the Three Scenarios

Main Exogenous Variables	Period	Three Scenarios		
		Optimistic	Baseline	Pessimistic
(1) Population growth rate	"12th Five-Year" (2011–2015)	Grow by 0.428% annually		
	"13th Five-Year" (2016–2020)	Grow by 0.311% annually		
	"14th Five-Year" (2012–2025)	Grow by 0.176% annually		
(2) Urbanisation rate (AIPP= Annual Increased Percentage Points)	"12th Five-Year" (2011–2015)	53.0% in 2015 (AIPP=1.1)	52.5% in 2015 (AIPP=1.0)	52.0% in 2015 (AIPP=0.9)
	"13th Five-Year" (2016–2020)	57.0% in 2020 (AIPP=0.8)	56.0% in 2020 (AIPP=0.7)	55.0% in 2020 (AIPP=0.6)
	"14th Five-Year" (2012–2025)	60.5% in 2025 (AIPP=0.7)	59.0% in 2025 (AIPP=0.6)	57.5% in 2025 (AIPP=0.5)
(3) Ratio of fiscal expenditure on education to GDP	"12th Five-Year" (2011–2015)	4.0%	3.5–4.0%	3.5–4.0%
	"13th Five-Year" (2016–2020)			
	"14th Five-Year" (2012–2025)		4.0%	

IV. Conclusions

In the face of the possible low growth rates of overseas developed economies and the gradual diminishing of the new domestic workforce, in order to realise an annual growth rate between 7.1 per cent and 8.6 per cent during 2011–2025 under the optimistic scenario, China should carry out the process of urbanisation and economic reform, increase the inputs in R&D and education, improve the TFP, further develop the tertiary industry, strive to expand consumption, upgrade the industrial structure, and improve the investment and consumption structure while expanding the size of the economy.

—Prof. Li Xuesong

Professor Li Xuesong in conversation with the former Governor-General of New Zealand, Sir Anand Satyanand.

A Faustian bargain

The road to perdition is littered with the figures of people who've tried to predict accurately what's going to happen over the next decade or so. But branching out from that, I guess most people accept, or have argued – in the Western world, anyway – that the Communist Party of China has had a kind of Faustian bargain with its people in the sense that, so long as there are high rates of economic growth, the creaky and unreconstructed nature of the political institutions of China can be left like that. And it's not just the World Bank and the State Council of Development Research Centre but others, in China and elsewhere, who are pointing out now that the likelihood is that growth will diminish over the next 10 years. It's also reasonably likely, I think, that many of the salient problems facing the Chinese leadership, and the new leadership, won't be solved. It's going to be much more reasonable for the leaders just to carry on more or less as they are, without having to tackle, wholesale, that list: fiscal and financial reforms, social welfare reforms so that domestic consumption can be improved, reduction in levels of corruption and environmental degradation, and so on.

The question really is, is the Chinese political system, and political structure, wholly stable?

The question I want to put is really the one issue that we haven't talked at all about today which is to do with politics. This week, just to take a random example, a deputy editor of Xuexi Shibao, which is a journal connected to the Central Party school in China, published an article in which he was critical – not praising, but critical – of the current Chinese leadership and singled out the failure to implement any form of democratisation as one of the most important features of what they haven't done right. The question really is, is the Chinese political system, and political structure, wholly stable? There are no signs of it coming apart at the seams despite the more sort of alarmist predictions. But there are many signs of restlessness or uneasiness, and many signs that it's a huge problem to cope with, dealing with this massive growth within China, with a population of 1.3 plus billion.

—*Peter Harris*

Upgrading industrial structures

In the future, China will still maintain its focus on the areas surrounding it. With economic readjustment, Chinese foreign trade is being downgraded, while industrial structures are being upgraded. So regional industrial structures will follow in this change and there may be more chances for Sino-New Zealand bilateral cooperation.

First, it will benefit new industrial cooperation, in areas such as the environment industry, animal husbandry and agriculture, according to the advantages each side has.

Second, it is the right time to develop industrial cooperation on the basis of trade relations. The aim is to go beyond trade relations and bilateral relations to have new industries in the region that are relevant to future regional and global demand.

Third, Sino-New Zealand cooperation has been associated with agriculture, the food industry, raw materials and some high technology. Some of these are sensitive and relate to national strategic interests. Therefore, we need to give more political and strategic consideration, and to devise long-term arrangements. So some national policies and the guidance offered will need more coordination.

Fourth, with more investment abroad, Chinese large-project investment is going to increase, in areas such as the environment, services, and the agricultural industry, in addition to energy and natural resources, in line with China's economic growth. There will be a need for practical technology relevant to upgrading Chinese industries in areas such as remote technology for medical treatment, education, management, agricultural technology, as well as mining, construction, transportation, dairy products and so on.

Fifth, New Zealand has mature systems for social management and open [governance]. That will be helpful for Chinese social reform and structural adjustment from the central to the local level.

—*Prof. Han Feng*

Keeping up

不进则退

If you don't go forward, you fall back

Maintaining relevance

A key question, looking forward to the next 40 years, is how can we maintain our relevance in China? If you think of China's 31 provinces as separate provincial economies, in 2001 Taiwan was the largest economy, and Hong Kong number two. Today Taiwan is equivalent to the fifth largest, while Hong Kong would be the 13th. In 2001 New Zealand's economy would have been in size equivalent to China's 9th largest province. Today New Zealand comes in at number 23, between Jilin and Yunnan. In five years time it is projected to have fallen to 25, between Jilin and Xinjiang. This metric conveys the degree of economic change in China, and the challenge New Zealand faces.

As China opened up New Zealand played an important role beyond our economic size, being opportunistically in the right place at the right time, and taking advantage of that. This is the story of the FTA. The question is how do we stay where we are, compete, and remain relevant, when over time our economy becomes the equivalent of a small Chinese province?

How do we stay where we are, compete, and remain relevant?

It's here relevant to consider why the reforms of the '70s and '80s in New Zealand did not deliver big dividends, while in China similar reforms have brought about huge changes. The conclusion of a number of studies is that the difference is the distance factor. New Zealand is just a long way away from the centres of economic action, and we are a long way from China. Looking forward, we need some clear, simple strategies.

These are areas we need to focus on:

- **Transport**. Air New Zealand has just cancelled its Beijing direct service. It's a simple thing, but over 10 years it will have a profound effect on how linked in New Zealand is with decision-makers in China. The Government owns 80 per cent of Air New Zealand; it should direct it to act in the national interest. Maintaining direct links with the capital of the largest economy in Asia would seem an obvious necessity if New Zealand is to compete.

- **Services** must take the lead in driving economic interaction. There was talk of New Zealand being a services hub. That has now fallen away, and yet the growth leader in China over the next 20 years will be the services sector. Natural History New Zealand is a great example of an exporter of services that has established a thriving business.
- **Investment**. There's a need to maintain a semblance of bilateral parity in terms of investment. New Zealand is constrained by its low savings rate, and its relative economic size and financial wealth, but we can and should invest in our human capital. We need to make sure our young people are able to compete with, and benefit from the rise of China. And that means investing in Chinese and Asian studies and languages. We have a long way to go, and much to do.

The future has risks for New Zealand. We tend to assume that the step change associated with the FTA will continue into the future. If it slows down, we'll have to adapt and reform in order to maintain the momentum in trade with China – in services as well as goods. The need for reform and change is also true of China as well; what has worked in the last 20 years may not work beyond the next few years. It is in New Zealand's interest to see a reinvigoration of reform in China.

—Rodney Jones

More challenges than opportunities

The economic relations between China and New Zealand have one special feature – the existence of an FTA between the two countries. But the discrepancies are significant. China's economic scale is very large – the second biggest in the world, and soon to become the biggest. The New Zealand economy will more and more become part of the value-added chain into China. You can see the process in Australia, where there is a mining boom to supply the China market. As China rises it will promote more and more investment in the dairy industry in New Zealand, and New Zealand will have a dairy boom like the Australian mining boom. Australia has in effect moved to a two-speed economy, and it may be we will see something of the same sort in New Zealand, with a decline in manufacturing and a boom in the dairy industry.

China's growth will provide some opportunities, but it will also provide some challenges. New Zealand will not be able to shut out localisation in China. Does New Zealand have enough excellent technology to compete in the China market? It may be able to hold its own in the dairy field, and perhaps it has at least some technology in other areas, but in all spheres? I'm uncertain whether New Zealand will have the technological capacity to get the upper hand in the China market. I'm optimistic about the future, but it will present big challenges – maybe more challenges than opportunities.

—Prof. Ding Dou

Six priority areas

If you identify an opportunity, seize it, and work hard, you can make it a reality. That's what we should do. There are six priority areas we could explore:

- **Dairy farming**. Fonterra can't supply China's needs. New Zealand could work harder to promote exchanges in this sector, and take advantage of the huge demand in China.
- **Food safety**. This is a key concern in China. What country is better placed to help than New Zealand?
- **Creative industries**. Hollywood is the number one overseas production centre for Chinese films – Wellington could be number two. In November 2003 a high-level Chinese film delegation visited New Zealand for the launching of The Lord of the Rings. Many blockbuster movies made in China have their post-production work done in Wellington.
- **Tourism**. The distance is not a big constraint. Many Chinese white-collar workers are now looking to travel overseas. Already China has become New Zealand's second biggest source of foreign tourists.
- **Education**. There are up to 40,000 Chinese students in New Zealand each year. Regular exchanges have been set up between Chinese and New Zealand universities.
- **Engagement on regional economic issues**. Work together towards economic integration in the Asia-Pacific region. New Zealand is not big but it is expert in developing trade. For instance, New Zealand has been a promoter of the Trans-Pacific Partnership. That is an interesting initiative, and when China wants to join we will need to learn from your expertise. New Zealand has become a member of the East Asia Summit, and China was among the first to enthusiastically endorse its participation. Now the ASEANs are promoting the possibility of a regional economic partnership that is very ambitious – a free trade zone covering the whole of Asia, giving rise to the biggest free trade area in the world. For China and New Zealand there is no choice – we have to get involved.

—Ambassador Chen Mingming

Rise above differences

We all hope, and we have the confidence to expect, that China–NZ relations in the second 40 years will be as successful as in the first. The world we live in is now undergoing an unprecedented and sweeping transformation, presenting us with both opportunities and challenges. As important Asia-Pacific countries and members of the UN, EAS, APEC and other international and regional organisations, China and NZ must work even more closely together in order to seize the opportunities effectively and better meet the challenges. Our comprehensive cooperation for mutual benefit will acquire new dimensions as we move forward. Driven by our shared desire for a peaceful, stable and prosperous Asia-Pacific and sustained by our pursuit of common interests, China and NZ can do still more in the next 40 years both for themselves and as good examples to other countries.

China is at the critical juncture of its development. The just concluded 18th Party Congress unveiled the latest vision of what China will be like in the immediate future and beyond. Simply put, China will, by 2020 or the Party's centennial, complete the building of a moderately prosperous society in all respects and set the nation firmly on the march to its great renewal. One specific target that has been cited often recently is to double people's income before the decade ends.

It is not an easy thing to do. Though already the world's second largest economy thanks to a double-digit annual growth for over 30 years, China remains a developing country by UN standards, with a per capita GDP that is only a fraction of that of developed countries and a long list of high hurdles on the road to progress. In China today, the problem of unbalanced, uncoordinated and unsustainable development is still salient and acute. Resources and environmental constraints are serious enough to make achieving higher GDP the old way increasingly difficult. Against this backdrop, the Chinese government has called for applying the scientific outlook on development and implementing the overall plan for promoting economic, political, cultural, social and ecological progress simultaneously.

How does the future China–NZ relationship fit into this picture? One of the reasons for China to develop with such a stunning speed is that it has always been very keen at drawing on the successful experience of other countries. New Zealand is one of these countries. While leading China in a wide range of areas of economic and social development, NZ has long caught the attention of the the relevant Chinese departments. For example, NZ experience with environmental protection, with social management and rule of law, with effective and clean government, with cultural diversity and enrichment, with innovation and marketisation of R&D achievements, with vocational education, with gender equality, and so on. China, in my view, needs to learn from NZ now and for a considerably long time to come. At the same time, the full potential of the China–NZ FTA is yet to be tapped. The two countries ought to be more conscious of their responsibility, that is to serve as a harbinger and pioneer for what two countries can do together if they rise above differences and go for win-win cooperation.

—*Zhang Yuanyuan*

An enormous opportunity

I think the simple solution is to set up a framework here in New Zealand so that it's easy to do business, and just let people get on with it. There's very little that you can do by standing round and having think-tanks and all this sort of thing. You've just got to get on with it, celebrate those who are achieving, and encourage those who are coming in and having a go. And I also think that we need to de-emphasise our incumbents. Our big heroes in New Zealand are often in our incumbent companies that have been around for a long time, doing things in the same way. That's good, and they can get on and do those things, but they don't need further encouragement to keep doing them. They will do them if they work and they won't if they don't.

It's in our language. You sit around and listen to a group of companies in New Zealand and they talk about export, or they talk about trade. These are economic terms – they're not business terms. What is exporting? We need businesses to be thinking about building relationships with customers, finding new things that create real value for consumers out there in the world.

I think the best thing you can do is make sure that you encourage these people and get out of their way.

China is just such an enormous opportunity. We should not be thinking about China as a country; we should be looking for the luxury opportunities for a country like New Zealand. The reality is that a lot of our consumables go into these places on a cost leadership model. That means we are the lowest price point in the market so that they buy the volume that we want to sell them. That will continue to go on for some time, but the great thing about the free trade agreement is that it has opened the door and it has removed barriers.

I think you'll see over the next 10 to 20 years that alongside the commodities new players will come in: they'll travel there, they'll built relationships, they'll catch up with their old university mates who they met here and they'll find opportunities to do things, and they'll do a whole lot of things that we just haven't even thought about at this time. So I think the best thing you can do is make sure that you encourage these people and get out of their way.

—John Penno

Stability and consistency

China is the biggest source of Australian migrants, number one now, followed by India. China is the biggest source of students, about 130,000 per year. China is our biggest trading partner, almost $130 billion last year. So it's twice your dependence, almost 28 per cent of our total. On the other side, Australia is among China's top ten sources of imports and it is the top destination for overseas investment. But, the closer we get through such transactions, the more that the context matters, the more that other issues emerge, the greater the strategic questions. . . . So a lesson really – the big lesson is stability and consistency is what China is looking for in such a relationship. And in the last few years we haven't always walked the talk, or talked the walk. We've appeared to say one thing and do another. We've swung around in following domestic focus groups. This has caused, I think, a hiccup in our relationship with China. I don't think it's an everlasting barrier, but I think the relationship is not as strong as it could be, or should be, and I think that's the big lesson. Stability of the relationship is important. It doesn't necessarily mean we have to agree, but consistency is essential.

Looking ahead, a note of caution. There's a presumption in both our countries that the more attention we pay to China, the closer we will get. But I believe there are limits to that closeness. Not on the personal side – I hope there are no limits to how close we get personally – but on the institutional side. The People's Republic is a very particular, all-enveloping party state. Its institutions have hardly changed at all in the 63 years of its existence. It is the most politicised country in the world. Domestic issues will always take priority. That's why right now people in China and those overseas who watch events there are absolutely focused on the leadership transition taking place, soon at the National Party Congress and next March completed at the National People's Congress.

My other cautionary note about the onward and upward presumptions about the relationship that both Australia and New Zealand face, is what if the new Xi Jinping Li Kecheng team is unable to produce the consensus among party factions required to introduce reforms, which have been long delayed and which the Hu Wen team were unable to introduce, particularly reforms in the finance sector with other sectors needed to shift the growth driver from investment and exports to domestic consumption and services. That will prove a testing time. If the transactional basis of the relationship starts to falter and the economy slows substantially, possibly even below the worst-case scenario that we heard just now.

I'm not saying it's going to happen, but I think we should prepare for that and make sure the relationship continues and is not based purely on transactional elements. There's some urgency about this question in Australia as we see our bigger new resource projects, like Olympic dam, begin to hit up already against the Chinese commodity slow-down with the loss of many projected jobs. Where will the relationship go now? It's also our 40th anniversary year and we don't yet have any convincing answers. The New Zealand–China relationship has flourished to a degree under the radar, but as it bulks up, challenges as well as opportunities will increase.

—Rowan Callick

A strategy for China

You definitely need a strategy if you're investing in China. You need a strategy if you're not investing in China. I was always surprised at how many people would come and see me and tell me that they wanted to do business in China. And when I asked them how many times they'd been to China, often it was none. And I'd say, well, go away for a year and visit it often and then come back and see me and we'll have another discussion. It wasn't just New Zealand companies; it was a lot of foreign companies who were chasing the apparent goldmine in China. A lot of people were falling over themselves to get on the bandwagon, and they weren't doing the work that they should have been doing before they got there.

Whether or not you're investing in China, you have to have a China strategy.

Another investment bank summed the strategy for China up pretty well, and that was that whatever China produces will go down in price and whatever it consumes will go up in price. If you took that as a simplistic way of what you need to understand in terms of dealing with China, that was a pretty good way of enunciating it.

In my view, and in a New Zealand context, whether or not you're investing in China, you have to have a China strategy, because China is the key variable in terms of pricing for almost anything globally now. Also it is the largest consumer at the margin for most things. And that is extremely important from New Zealand's point of view. So, at a government level, I think we need a strategy and it needs to be a much longer-term strategy than what we currently have. And at a business level we need to have strategies for China, and again that's whether or not you're going to actually do business in China.

I think a lot of New Zealand companies are better placed not to actually do business in China, but to do business in other countries in Asia who happen to be impacted by what China was doing. It's a lot easier to get into other countries in Asia who will clearly be impacted by what China is doing but where there are opportunities from a New Zealand company point of view at the smaller level. New Zealand might be better suited to meeting those opportunities than to try and grow a more holistic strategy in China.

I think the other reason for understanding the strategy around China is: what are the really big drivers in terms of what is happening in China? When you look back to what happened in America with the baby boomer population between 1946 and 1964, that was effectively 80 million people. And the key difference for those baby boomers was that, unlike their parents' generation who had been through the Great Depression and the Second World War, the baby boomer population were confident about the future. They felt better about the future and because of that, they were prepared to borrow against future income. They basically felt things were going to get better, not worse. And that led to a growth in consumption, and it was a consumption boom that certainly fuelled the American economy, and also fuelled the global economy pretty much all the way through to the global financial crisis.

The key aspect of that boom was not just those 80 million people, it was what was happening there. It was largely to do with household development, so as the demographics of the population changed, household growth exceeded population growth. Household growth in the US through from the Second World War to the mid-70s when it peaked at about two and a half per cent, outgrew population growth which was about one per cent. So the total number of houses grew faster than the population. The average number of people per house fell, but the number of appliances, be it TVs, washing machines or whatever, grew because household formation grew.

Now you apply that to China, apply that to Asia, the equivalent demographic in Asia is about a billion people. Eighty million people in the baby boomer population in the US, about a billion people in China. And one of the key drivers there is urbanisation growth rate. So what is happening in China is that the movement of people to urban areas is happening at a rate that is quicker than any other country in history and also happening on a scale that is larger than any other country in history.

When the UK went through a period of rapid industrialisation in the mid-1800s there were about six million people living in the UK. In China it's 1.3 billion people. In the 1980s less than 20 per cent of the population lived in urban areas. Under the 12th five-year plan, ratified last year, they aim to see that number grow to 51 per cent of the population. By 2050 it'll be 80 per cent of the population. That's an unbelievable shift. The world has never seen it before. And that throws up enormous issues in terms of consumption, pollution, water usage and so on.

From New Zealand's point of view, you have to understand that if you're going to do business in China. But you also have to understand it if you're not doing business in China, because that will be the single biggest driver in terms of growth globally. New Zealand needs to understand it, and we don't spend enough time strategising about that future.

—*Rob Morrison*

Falling in love

> *If we regard China's needs and interests as as vital as our own needs and interests, and search for mutually productive solutions, we can do it I don't doubt.*

One of the earlier panellists today said that to get anywhere, you've got to fall in love with China. I think that it's hard to attribute the behaviours of individuals to the behaviours of nations, but I think that love really means that the two parties concerned must give each other's interests an equal status with their own. And understand what the other needs and wants, and give that just as much importance as their own needs and wants. And I think if we do that, and we think about, for example, the imbroglio of the Crafar farms, that if we were to think and get our people to realise what it is that China needs – which is security of supply of trustworthy foods – and what we need – which is security of access to the world's great markets – if we think of things in that way instead of dividing the world into black hats and white hats, we can then quite readily find mutually satisfactory arrangements. And I think that is a real lesson. If we regard China's needs and interests as as vital as our own needs and interests, and search for mutually productive solutions, we can do it I don't doubt.

—*Jim Sutton*

Difficult foreign policy choices

对症下药

Choose a medicine to suit the illness

Our core foreign policy task for the next 20 years (I take Australia to be quasi-domestic, or at least sororal, business) is managing China's management of us. The first Chinese scrabbled for the residual specks of gold, and discriminatory laws kept them for 100 years in the margins. Their great-great-grandchildren and their children are professionals and businesspeople. The next Chinese were students and bolt-holers and they generated an anti-Asian populist party. The Chinese come now as lenders and owners, buyers and sellers and, in the future, gentle and not-so-gentle adapters and adjusters of our systems.

We have a choice in how we manage China's management of us. We can huddle in with Australia and the United States, determinedly peripheral. Americans are kin (mostly). Chinese are not. Or we can choose independence, our default positioning ever since the United States and Australia kicked us out of the alliance for refusing to play with some of their lethal toys.

> *Our core foreign policy task of the next 20 years is managing China's management of us.*

If we choose the first option, we may find the Chinese less welcoming and less willing to fix behind-the-border issues for us that smooth our path to its enriching consumers, though that may be overstated. But we may get compensating, or part-compensating, deals from the Americans and be able to run a smaller and less deft foreign service by largely cruising on their initiatives and their (and the Australians') analysis and think-tanks. We may also find common cause in Southeast and South Asian capitals to the degree that they want a counterbalance to China's power.

If we choose the independence option, we will need to be agile, innovative, active, persistent and resilient. That will imply investing much more heavily in our foreign service and in our connections with other countries' governments, think-tanks and business organisations. Independence would help, though not guarantee, to keep us sweet with China. If promoted with skill, independence can give us a degree of very soft influence as an honest broker and active participant in multilateral systems. It can win friends in Southeast and South Asia.

My guess is that, despite the Americaphilia in the current cabinet, it will not bend the independent foreign policy line so far as to "take sides". The next Labour-led cabinet will reaffirm the independence line and the next generation of National

MPs will be comfortable with it – though looking out beyond 2020 is hazardous because there will be much potential for intra-state and inter-state tension in Asia.

—*Colin James*

Understanding is crucial

New Zealand's relationship with China is not special, but relations in the past have been really good, and looking towards the future they will continue to be good – even better than in the past.

It has to be recognised that things are changing – not just in the bilateral relationship, but also regionally in the Asia-Pacific. We should not focus on our selfish interests – we will each play a different role but there are many areas where we can cooperate within the region.

China itself is changing. China will continue to rise, and its investment in New Zealand will continue to increase. New Zealand has to be prepared for the fact that it will see more Chinese investment in New Zealand, and more Chinese people in New Zealand. That increased attention will be a good thing, but it will spark a lot of discussion. Most Chinese companies are preparing to go outside China and become global entities. That's a natural process – you've seen the same story in other Asian economies.

Dealing with rising powers is not an easy thing, especially with a rising China.

We are two quite different states, but we can share understanding. Understanding is sometimes very difficult to describe, but understanding is crucial. New Zealand offers a good example for other Western countries in dealing with a rising power. For example, we worked together on a research report on how to cooperate in the South Pacific, and presented it to the Pacific Islands Forum. The results can now be seen – we found a way forward. It is possible to cooperate instead of engaging in rivalry.

Dealing with rising powers is not an easy thing, especially with a rising China. China's rise has been too fast, and too big. The future offers a big, big challenge – China will be first, but India and Brazil will come along later. I recall at Davos an elderly American lady said to me that China's rise was a good thing, but Americans weren't sure that it was a good thing for the United States. The US benefited from the post–World War II world order: "We never expected such a good life. But our grandchildren may not enjoy the same good life".

The world has changed China. We have had to deal with integration into the international community, opening up and reform. That has all been such a big change for China. But now people are starting to speak of China changing the world. No one can be quite sure what China's future will be, the change has been so fast.

China insists that it will pursue peaceful development. That's different from former rising powers. People aren't willing to believe fully in that – they want to wait and see. There are rising tensions between China and its neighbours over disputed islands. How will that be handled? I'm reasonably optimistic China won't use military force, but will handle matters in a way that avoids confrontation. We need some time. There's rising concern about how to handle these emerging disputes, but also a rising consensus that we have to find a way out. China needs peaceful development. The new leadership is insisting on peaceful development, to make China a prosperous country.

—Zhang Yunling

An interesting tension

Is China going to be dominated by big power relationships? Of course. The major relationship in the region we live in, the Asia Pacific, is going to be between the United States, which is the currently dominant power, and China, which is the rising power. That creates an interesting tension for New Zealand, with its long-term traditional and cultural relationships with the United States, and its contemporary close relationship with China and the importance of the Chinese trading relationship, which in fact last year exceeded that of the trade with the United States.

—Phil Goff

Restlessness

I want to make a point about these conversations people are having about the zero-sum game between China and America. The fear is that we will have to deal with tensions, with stresses, we will have to be very nimble, whereas my own view is that we have a long way to go yet before we really have to be concerned about that. Even close working relations with the United States, and close working relations with China, are compatible for some time to come. It's not a fashionable view at the moment, especially since the new American pivot back to the Asia-Pacific, which has caused some deep concern for China. But it is, I believe, one that's defensible and I alluded briefly to the thinking behind it when I mentioned that in point of fact, relations between China and the United States have been more peaceful and positive in most respects in the last 10 years than they were for previous decades.

—Peter Harris

Nuanced answers

The pivot may not be entirely negative; the pivot may be positive. I think it's quite good that the US is paying more attention to the Asia-Pacific region, and it may have benevolent results at the moment because of the South China Sea confrontations that are causing some realignments – temporary realignments maybe – amongst Southeast Asian countries that are looking to America for support. But this may not be a permanent thing. We see America has this regular strategic economic dialogue

Here are some questions about China and its implications for this pimple of a society and economy over the next 20 years:

1. What will be the trajectory of China's society, and therefore its politics, through the next 20 years as its middle class expands and enriches and travels the world of ideas and images through cyberspace? What tension will there be between haves and have-nots and between the privileged and the non-privileged and what form will it take? Will there still be endemic and corrosive corruption in 20 years? How fast and deep will China develop social security, decent labour conditions and wages, and equitable access to health, housing and education?
2. What will be the trajectory of China's economy through the next 20 years as its dynamic expansion and integration into the global trading and financial systems stretches autocrats' and bureaucrats' capacity to manage it? When at some point, or points, it goes into recession, will the banking and support systems cope? How will demographic change impact on economic capability? How will the new generation of production technologies affect its competiveness and capacity to generate enriching employment?
3. Looking out over the next 20 years, will China rely more on soft power than hard power in its international dealings in trade and security or will hard power at some point prevail as its economic strength or, conversely, its need for fuel, minerals and water, emboldens it? Can it manage North Korea's reintegration? How will it treat Japan? Will it see India as a rival or an also-ran? Will it respect international and multilateral institutions and abide by their rulings when they are unfavourable? Or will it stick with its strong line on the inviolability of national sovereignty? If the second, will that slow or reverse its global integration?

3a. Might China by 2032 become the big, bad guy – the new coloniser – as a result of its aggressive drive for resources and food (that is, land and water) across the world?

3b. Will New Zealand stick to its independent foreign policy line?

4. What will China's role in the South Pacific be through the next 20 years? How will it influence what New Zealand does there? How will the United States and Australia respond?
5. How quickly will China build capacity to generate new science and new or adapted technologies? How will that affect its treatment of intellectual property? Will it genuinely develop and adopt environment-friendly technologies?
6. How will New Zealand – and Aoteoroa – respond to the Chinese state and private companies' bid to own more of our productive capacity, supply chains and access to water (that is, land)? Will New Zealand become increasingly dependent on Chinese funds for its equity and private and public borrowing?

6a. What will be the role of Chinese in New Zealand – New Zealand Chinese – vis-à-vis China? Will they be a bridge into China and from China into New Zealand? And can we make use of the alumni, those who studied here?

7. Assuming more Chinese involvement in our economy over the next 20 years, how will we manage increasing migration pressure? Will we in 50 years have been in effect recolonised?
8. Will Australia's responses to those questions about China's ownership and migration be a constraining or influential factor in how we can and do respond?
9. Will this country sometime wake up to the point that children and adults should get to know Chinese history and culture and be fluent in mandarin? Or will that happen when Chinese residents here bring it about?

—*Colin James*

with China, very close relations at the top levels, and I'm not so bothered. Hugh White, an Australian Defence Department Deputy Secretary from before, now a Professor at ANU, has produced first of all an essay, now a whole book, raising it into a zero-sum game. Either we're for China or we're for the United States. He does this well, he raises the debate, but it's unnecessary to follow him in his alternatives. I think there are more nuanced answers. . . .

The leadership in China knows what's happening. Knowing isn't necessarily management, and I think as new generations emerge in China who have grown up in comparative well-being, who don't feel especially grateful to the Party for the growth in living standards, they will actually – to an extent – credit their parents and so on with the circumstances in which they are living. While they won't necessarily reject the Party, they won't give it due deference for having brought those five hundred million we're hearing about out of poverty, which is indeed a wonderful thing. And it will be that much harder for the leadership to work out a new form of legitimacy to take the place of that deal that Deng Xiaoping carved out after Mao. I'm not sure what new form of legitimacy the Party will devise for itself. I think that's a really big challenge.

—*Rowan Callick*

Peter Harris speaks from the floor at the Wellington symposium.

Handling sudden changes

> *The sorts of uncertainties that sudden changes in complex systems can bring don't absolve you from trying to be strategic.*

Human societies are complex adaptive systems, if I can quote Neil Ferguson. And so are the artifacts of human societies, and therefore you can have quite sudden, dramatic changes. One of my favorites is the First World War: an archduke was shot and massive change followed which no one predicted. People had predicted tension, and maybe a small war, a short war, but no one predicted anything like what happened. We've just had an example in the financial system – the GFC – and we're still going through that. So, projecting forward what will happen in China, you have to bear in mind that it might well be some dramatic change regarding which we can't forecast when it will happen, or what will trigger it, or what form it will take. And just to say that the sorts of uncertainties that sudden changes in complex systems can bring don't absolve you from trying to be strategic. There's quite a good recent paper by the Boston Consulting Group which discusses how you can prepare yourself to the maximum to try and handle sudden changes that you hadn't envisaged. And that really comes down to resilience, where you need quite a strong core but an adaptable surround to that core. And I think that is the sort of approach we will need to take to our foreign affairs generally over the next 20 years, and as a big part of that, to China.

—*Colin James*

A mix of relationships

There are two really interesting questions. First, how can New Zealand businesses get the most out of the commercial environment? I think that's reflected as well in the government's China Inc Strategy, which is really about making the most of those opportunities. To some extent, without being too crude about it, it's about maximising the situation. It would be hard to make a case that New Zealand's relationship with China could become way, way too close for comfort, unless we felt that we were becoming so over-reliant upon China that it was giving us an unbalanced trade profile. But it seems to me you can maximise a range of commercial relationships simultaneously. Of course, capacity constraints and other things would get in the way. But on the whole, most people would say more is better.

When it comes to that second question, about the political and strategic relationships, it seems to me that maximising approaches fall away fairly quickly. Because it's more likely that attempts to maximise one relationship at the political, and particularly the strategic level, will have an impact on other relationships. That doesn't mean you're in a zero-sum game. It doesn't necessarily mean that you face quite the choice of going either with an independent approach or becoming a client of the United States. I think the benefit of that sort of analysis is that it gives us the two ends of the spectrum, although you could go even further and say beyond an independent approach you might actually have a situation where you do choose China as your major sole partner politically, economically and strategically.

At what point are we willing to be in a position where we can't please both, but we actually have to displease both of the big powers at certain times?

I don't expect that to happen in New Zealand's case any time soon. So what it comes down to is thinking about the relationship in terms of at what point are we willing to modify other relationships to benefit the China relationship? But it also means at what point are we willing to modify elements of the China political and strategic relationship to benefit other relationships? And that's not because any relationship that we have is worth working for in its own right. It's just that there's a particular mix of relationships that seem to me to suit where New Zealand wants to be positioned. You come back to subordinating all of those relationships to that desirable mix, which I think we as a country do need to keep reminding ourselves of.

It does mean a positioning that is much more than a commercial positioning. We need to try to put the China relationship into a rounder and bigger context, recognising that the enormous change in China, and the economic drivers that has produced, are the big story of the last 30 or so years, and not to be ignored. There are obvious issues that come up in terms of what we are willing to do for other relationships as they affect the China relationship. Of course, the US relationship is one of the big things in regional politics. There is a question there about whether it makes sense to think about the US relationship as one type of relationship focused very much around history and cultural affinity and common values and the security side of the relationship, and the China relationship as a more recent one based largely around the commercial impulse and common interests deriving from that.

But of course those two things are coming together. China is not part of the TPP. And I think Trade Minister Tim Groser and others are on record as saying that New Zealand would not sign up to a TPP that was seen to exclude China as a potential member. So that's a sign of those two worlds coming together. The United States is getting more involved in Asia's economic integration, which has sometimes been seen as China's paddock, and China by virtue of the political and strategic implications of the economic rise is becoming more involved in Asia's security, which is traditionally seen as America's paddock. That interaction is something that we need to deal with, and that also reduces the chance that we can maximise both relationships.

It's also about a very, another very, very important relationship that New Zealand has, and that's the relationship we have with Australia. If Australia does take a position in terms of its relationship with the US that continues to move closer and closer in a strategic partnership, and that seems to be where it is going, and if Australia also has expectations about where New Zealand fits in that, then that may mean that the biggest impact of where the US and China go will be actually in terms of New Zealand's interaction with Australia.

Dealings with Australia are already an interesting consideration, let alone our relationships with the ASEAN countries and the various regional organisations that they are at the centre of. In a sense, that's really the main point. At what point are we willing to be in a position where we can't please both, but we actually have to displease both of the big powers at certain times? It's not likely to be a once and for all choice – one moment where we have to make that big decision. Rather, there are likely to be a number of smaller choices along the way. And it gets back to a point made earlier today about the value of nimbleness. That's really going to continue to be important, and that's something where I think we need to work very, very hard on.

—*Prof. Rob Ayson*

An asymmetrical equation

The first session raised the question of how sustainable the equation of strong economy and weak politics that has to a large degree applied to our relations so far is. It could right itself, it could endure, it could lead to some sort of crisis. If we look at case studies, I think such an equation may not be sustainable. We can't just have very asymmetrical development with one leg strong, and the other leg very small and thin.

The case at hand is China/Japan relations. These relations are usually characterised as hot economy and chilly politics. What is happening now, if we look at the pressure of nationalism over the Senkoku/Diaoyu islands, I think unfortunately that relations have never been tenser between Beijing and Tokyo. Some people have speculated that China/Japan relations now are edging to the verge of war. So the equation of such a strong economy and weak politics can definitely never endure.

But is there any way for us to get out of the situation, or to have some sort of therapy to get our relations well balanced between politics and economy? In the short- to medium-term I can see nothing. Such an equation will go on. The reason is simple. First of all, we have a lot of structural constraints. There is a lot of concern about the future of China, a lot of concern about China's domestic transformation, a lot of concern about some sort of lack of cultural affinity to bond the two sides as strongly as New Zealand with the UK or US.

The second thing is of course New Zealand. I have really felt, since I got here, that you are very nice, considerate, moderate guys. But the problem is, you are part of the West. China is foreign. A lot of people have talked about language learning, but it seems to me the most important way for Kiwis to know China better is through history. We are a country of 3,000 years history. You are a country of less than 200. It's not just some sort of different historical roots. What is most important is we have a totally different historical view and historical background, in almost every way. So we have to face up to this constraint. There is no way to escape; there is no way to gloss over it.

You are very nice, considerate, moderate guys. But the problem is, you are part of the West.

I am less concerned about the sustainability of such an equation. Even if it is asymmetrical I think it could persist. I have two reasons. One is look at Chinese and New Zealanders. What sort of force eventually gets us together? I think the reason is very, very simple. We share a lot because we are in the same category. Because no matter that you are Kiwi, and we are Chinese, we are very utilitarian. Our countries happen to be trading powers. The leading philosophy for such contacts, now they are getting bigger and more massive, is material realism. This motive is always there, it never loses steam. So I am very optimistic. Whenever some sort of new crisis comes along I don't think we have to be too pessimistic about our political relationship. When we heard Prime Minister John Key's presentation this morning, I have never been more encouraged. Kiwis are cool-headed, you are very pragmatic, and you know how to build friendly relations. If we can have this, that's enough.

Second point. I couldn't agree more that New Zealand needs a China strategy. But in my view, if New Zealand is to successfully form a China strategy, you will have to clarify what kind of strategic bearings you have with regard to China, and what sort of consent exists among your elites about China. If you can do that, I am sure you will have a persistent and broadly appealing China strategy. Let me give you my impressions about what key points could underlie our strategic bearing. The most important is that we should have insurmountable conviction, no matter how different we are. No matter how much we argue, the problem is that we are in the same boat in this century. If the boat sinks, you are gone, we are gone. If we can steer the boat into some very good sea navigation lane, then we will jointly have a better future. Such a conviction truly is a very strong underlying foundation for us to sustain our relations.

—Prof. Zhu Feng

CHINA SYMPOSIUM 2012

40 YEARS OF NZ-CHINA RELATIONS

To mark the 40th Anniversary of the Establishment of New Zealand-China Diplomatic Relations

5 September 2012, Wellington

4 December 2012, Beijing

PROGRAMME, Wellington

5 September 2012

8–8.40am **Arrival and Registration**

9–9.30am Introduction **Prof. Pat Walsh,** Vice Chancellor, Victoria University of Wellington

Keynote Speech **Rt. Hon. John Key,** Prime Minister

9.30–10.55am **The NZ–China Partnership: 40 years of Politics and Diplomacy**

Convenor: **Rt. Hon. Sir Don McKinnon,** Chair, New Zealand China Council

Speakers: **Chris Elder,** Former New Zealand Ambassador to China; **Prof. Han Feng,** Deputy Director, National Institute of International Strategy, CASS

Panel: **Hon. Phil Goff,** Member of Parliament, Labour Party Foreign Affairs spokesperson; **Dr Jian Yang,** Member of Parliament, National Party; **Peter Harris,** Senior Fellow, Centre for Strategic Studies, Victoria University of Wellington, former Ford Foundation Representative in China

10.55–11.10am **Morning tea**

11.10am–12.30pm **The Social Impact: Migration, Education and Culture**

Convenor: **Prof. Brian Moloughney,** Pro Vice Chancellor of Humanities, University of Otago

Speaker: **Prof. Manying Ip,** Professor of Asian Studies, University of Auckland

Panel: **Michael Stedman,** Managing Director, Natural History New Zealand; **Liyang Ma,** Manager, Auckland office, Asia New Zealand Foundation; **Charles Finny,** Chair, Education New Zealand

12.30–1.30pm **Lunch**

1.30–3pm **The Economic Relationship: Realising the Potential of the FTA**

Convenor: **Fran O'Sullivan**; Columnist, New Zealand Herald

Speakers: **Tony Alexander,** Publisher, Growing with China; **Dr Ma Tao,** Assistant Research Fellow, Institute of World Economics and Politics, CASS

Panel: **Richard Yan,** Founder, Chairman and Chief Executive Officer, Richina Group of companies; **John Penno,** Chief Executive Officer, Synlait Milk Ltd; **Jamie Tuuta,** Māori Trustee; **Girol Karacaoglu,** Chief Economist and Deputy Secretary, The Treasury

3–3.15pm **Afternoon tea**

3.15–4.40pm **Where to from here? New Challenges for New Zealand and China**

Convenor: **Tony Browne,** Chair, NZ Contemporary China Research Centre, Former Ambassador to China

Speakers: **Prof. Li Xuesong,** Deputy Director, Institute of Quantitative and Technical Economics, CASS; **Colin James,** Political journalist and analyst. Senior Associate, Institute of Governance & Policy Studies, Victoria University of Wellington.

Panel: **Rowan Callick,** Asia-Pacific editor, The Australian; **Rob Morrison,** Former Chairman and CEO Hong Kong–based CLSA Asia-Pacific Markets; **Prof. Robert Ayson,** Professor of Strategic Studies and Director, Centre for Strategic Studies, Victoria University of Wellington

4.40–5pm **Summary**

Prof. Zhu Feng, Deputy Director, Center for International & Strategic Studies (CISS), Peking University; **Brian Lynch,** Director, New Zealand Institute of International Affairs (NZIIA), 2003 to 2012

5–6.30pm **Reception** Hosted by **John Hayes MP**

Comments by **HE Ambassador Xu Jianguo**

日程PROGRAMME, Beijing

2012年12月4日 4 December, 2012

中国社会科学院第一学术报告厅 (北京市东城区建内大街5号)

Conference Hall, 1st Floor, Chinese Academy of Social Sciences, 5 Jianguomennei Dajie, Beijing

09:00–09:30 开幕式 **Opening Ceremony**

主持人: 李向阳, 中国社科院亚太与全球战略研究院 院长 研究员

Chair: Professor Li Xiangyang, Director-General, National Institute of International Strategy, CASS

主旨发言 Keynote Speeches:

黄浩涛 中国社会科学院 秘书长

Huang Haotao, Secretary General, Chinese Academy of Social Sciences

尼尔·奎格利, 惠灵顿维多利亚大学 常务副校长 教授

Professor Neil Quigley, Deputy Vice Chancellor, Victoria University of Wellington

09:30–11:00 中新外交关系40年

40 Years of Diplomatic Relations between China and New Zealand

主持人: 道格拉斯·克迪爵士, 新西兰国际事务研究所 主席

Chair: Sir Douglas Kidd, President, New Zealand Institute of International Affairs

发言人 Speakers:

陈明明, 中国驻新西兰前大使(2001–2005)

Chen Mingming, Chinese Ambassador to New Zealand (2001–2005)

艾尔德, 新西兰驻中国前大使(1993–1998)

Chris Elder, NZ Ambassador to China(1993–1998)

张援远,中国驻新西兰前大使(2006–2008)

Zhang Yuanyuan, Chinese Ambassador to New Zealand (2006–2008)

包逸之, 新西兰驻中国前大使(2004–2009)

Tony Browne, New Zealand Ambassador to China (2004–2009)

伍开文，新西兰驻中国大使

Carl Worker, New Zealand Ambassador to China

11:00–11:20 上午茶 **Morning Tea**

11:20–12:50 中国，新西兰和亚太地区安全与合作

Security and Cooperation in the Asia-Pacific between China and New Zealand

主持人：周云帆，中国社会科学院国际合作局 副局长

Chair: Zhou Yunfan, Deputy Director-General, Bureau of International Cooperation, CASS

发言人 Speakers:

张蕴岭，中国社会科学院国际研究学部 主任 研究员

Professor Zhang Yunling, Director, Academic Division of International Studies, CASS

付恩莱，新西兰外交通商部亚洲地区司 主任

Clare Fearnley, Director, Asia Regional Division, Ministry of Foreign Affairs and Trade

韩锋，中国社科院亚太与全球战略研究院 副院长 研究员

Professor Han Feng, Deputy Director-General, National Institute of International Strategy, CASS

兰马克，新西兰当代中国研究中心 高级研究员

Marc Lanteigne, Senior Research Fellow, NZ Contemporary China Research Centre

评论人 Discussants:

时永明，中国国际问题研究所南太平洋研究中心 副主任

Shi Yongming, Deputy Director, Centre for South Pacific Studies, China Institute of International Studies.

黄小明，新西兰当代中国研究中心 主任 教授

Professor Xiaoming Huang, Director, NZ Contemporary China Research Centre

12:50–14:00 午餐 **Lunch**

14:00–15:30 中新社会、文化、教育关系

Social, Cultural and Education Relations between China and New Zealand

主持人: 韩锋, 中国社科院亚太与全球战略研究院 副院长 研究员

Chair: Professor Han Feng, Deputy Director-General, National Institute of International Strategy, CASS

发言人 Speakers:

陈雯, 新西兰国家博物馆国际部 主任

Wen Powles, Director, International Affairs, Te Papa, Museum of New Zealand

刘树森, 北京大学新西兰中心 主任 教授

Professor Liu Shusen, Director, New Zealand Centre at Peking University

史达民, 新西兰自然历史公司 董事总经理

Michael Stedman, Natural History NZ

评论人 Discussants:

唐浩, 奥克兰大学亚洲学系 教授

Paul Clark, School of Asian Studies, University of Auckland

郭春梅, 中国现代国际关系研究院南亚东南亚和大洋洲研究所 副研究员

Guo Chunmei, Associate Professor, Institute of South & Southeast Asian & Oceanian Studies, China Institutes Of Contemporary International Relations

15:30–15:50 下午茶 **Afternoon Tea**

15:50–17:20 中新经贸投资关系的发展与前景

Development and Prospects of Economic, Trade and Investment Relations between China and New Zealand

主持人: 黄小明, 新西兰当代中国研究中心 主任 教授

Chair: Professor Xiaoming Huang, Director, NZ Contemporary China Research Centre

发言人 Speakers:

裴长洪，中国社会科学院经济研究所 所长 研究员

Professor Pei Changhong, Director-General, Institute of Economics, CASS

杨安廉，新西兰国家贸易发展局驻北京贸易代表

Alan Young, Trade Commissioner, New Zealand Trade and Enterprise

李雪松，中国社会科学院数量经济研究所 副所长 研究员

Li Xuesong, Deputy Director-General, Institute of Quantitative and Technical Economics, CASS

杨杰生，新西兰当代中国研究中心 研究员

Jason Young, Research Fellow, NZ Contemporary China Research Centre

评论人 Discussants:

周荣，新西兰威港资本咨询有限公司北京代表处 首席代表

Rodney Jones, Principal, Wigram Capital Advisors

马涛，中国社会科学院世界经济与政治研究所 副研究员

Ma Tao, Associate Professor, Institute of World Economics and Politics, CASS

丁斗，北京大学国际关系学院 副教授

Ding Dou, Associate Professor, School of International Studies, Peking University

17:20–17:50 会议总结 Conclusion

主持人：包逸之，新西兰当代中国研究中心顾问委员会 主席

Chair: Tony Browne, Chair, Advisory Board, NZ Contemporary China Research Centre

布莱安·林奇 新西兰国际事务研究所 所长

Brian Lynch, Director, NZ Institute of International Affairs

李向阳，中国社科院亚太与全球战略研究院 院长 研究员

Professor Li Xiangyang, Director-General, National Institute of International Strategy, CASS

18:00–20:00 晚宴 Dinner